The
Pressures
of
Teaching

The
Pressures
of
Teaching

How Teachers
Cope with
Classroom
Stress

MAUREEN PICARD ROBINS, EDITOR

PUBLISHING

New York

© 2010 by Maureen Picard Robins

Published by Kaplan Publishing, a division of Kaplan, Inc.
1 Liberty Plaza, 24th Floor
New York, NY 10006

Printed in the United States of America

10 9 8 7 6 5 4 3 2 1

Library of Congress Cataloging-in-Publication Data has been applied for.

ISBN: 978-1-4277-9966-1

Kaplan Publishing books are available at special quantity discounts to use for sales promotions, employee premiums, or educational purposes. For more information or to purchase books, please call the Simon & Schuster special sales department at 866-506-1949.

DEDICATION

To Wayne, Liz and Jackie, my reason for being

To Sid Trubowitz and Paul Longo for opening the
door when I knocked, who saw me for what I
was and made me (finally!) see it too

And, thanks, Mom.

CONTENTS

INTRODUCTION

LAST FRIDAY NIGHT my family dined at a favorite restaurant. The week had been hectic for all of us and we were grateful to relax together for a change. When I brought up the topic of school for dinner discussion, my husband said, "You're with your family now; leave work at work." Well, okay. As we left the restaurant, a group of teenagers ambled by us, then stopped, and turned around. My family didn't know what was happening. It was dark. What was up with these kids?

"Mrs. Robins!" they cried and surrounded me. They reached their arms out to hug me and then paused, realizing that a hug might not be proper, and instead engaged my hands in a midair mashing of high fives and handshakes. They all began talking at once (so much for my training them at the art of conversation and taking turns). It went something like this:

"I haven't been absent once this year!"

"I have a B-plus average!"

"See, Mrs. Robins, I'm doing fine!"

"I'm still reading books!"

Over the last year when not reading their notebooks or asking about books they'd read, my conversations with them—admittedly largely one-sided and, often, with a parent present—had sounded something akin to this:

"Set aside your anger and leave a corner of your brain for learning!"

"No one is going to call home when you don't do your homework in high school!"

"Please set more than one alarm clock so you can get to school on time!"

"This is the time when I test you and you test yourself to see if you can do this thing called 'school' on your own!"

"Think! I want you to think!"

Or my favorite, a teacher's classic remark, "What were you thinking? Or, was it that you weren't thinking at all?!"

Sometimes in the life of a teacher, school is family and family talks about school. It's exhausting just thinking about this. Most of the adults I know are allowed the luxury of choosing work as their sanctuary from the prying, critical eyes of often self-absorbed teenagers. Teaching is a profession that sends adults into the secret world of children and adolescents, sometimes in the role of first responders, where discipline, patience, and rationality are clearly in short supply. The myriad of student character types alone can be overwhelming, as Tim Clifford, a middle school English language arts teacher, describes in his essay *The Witch Trick: Becoming More than a One-Trick Pony.* High school math teacher Sandra Cohen quotes a colleague in her essay *The Pressures of Teaching* as saying, "We're like monkeys in a zoo. You stand in front of a class and students say terrible, mean things to you and you just have to wipe it off your face and come back the next day and act like it never happened."

Teaching can be exhausting and it can also be exhilarating, courageous, and breathtaking, but it is always challenging. Teaching is a profession that demands one person play many roles: parent, artist, actor, conciliator, problem solver, public speaker, mediator, inspirational speaker, psychiatrist, writer, manipulator, lifelong learner, party planner, disciplinarian, omniscient expert, generalist, role model, limitless source of patience and calmness, chief goal-setter, and nurturer. Teachers are decision makers. The researcher Madelyn Hunter, author of *Mastery Teaching: Increasing Instructional Effectiveness in Elementary and Secondary Schools,* wrote, "Teaching can be defined as a constant stream of professional decisions made before, during and after interaction with the student."

Still, many teachers believe they are among the most disrespected profession. *Education Week* recently reported results from a survey conducted by researchers at Public Agenda: "Based on their individual characteristics and attitudes about the profession, teachers naturally fell into three broad categories, which the researchers call the 'Disheartened,' 'Contented,' and 'Idealists.' Research reveals that those classified as 'disheartened,' hold the view that teaching is so demanding, it's a wonder that more people don't burn out." Teachers reported "high levels of frustration about the school administration, disorder in the classroom, and an undue focus on testing."

Indeed, in the 16 essays that follow, teacher-writers have addressed the demanding issues of disruptive behavior, disagreeable parents, race, lack of motivation, and the difficulties involved in teaching special education and English as a second language. There is anger and push-back from teachers who believe that teaching to or for the test has transformed a rich, energetic curriculum into one that is unappealing, superficial, and that fails to motivate the student or the educator.

While these teachers write about how the No Child Left Behind federal law has transformed their classrooms, they also talk about what they know is not—and perhaps cannot be—measured. They know that what is really learned is often evidenced much later, and may come informally, through a conversation between a teacher and her former students that begins, "Remember when you said..."

Invisible pressures are also in evidence in this anthology. Teachers often feel the persistent internal pressure to keep on learning, keep on developing as a teacher, and share with kids what they'll need to know in a future that most of us really can't imagine. Another invisible pressure is the "universal student engagement with each other by text messaging"? and other wireless communication.

The pressure of technology seems infused in everything. Technology makes the data easy to collect and the power of the technology allows us to individualize learning, but this exists within the confines of an educational system that was developed during the Industrial Revolution of the 18th and 19th centuries. In the 21st century, information is the fastest increasing quantity on this planet, and yet while many call this the "information" age, others insist it is the age of disinformation.

Several themes emerge from this enormously varied collection of essays. Some of the teachers' essays reflect back (as teachers often do) to when they were in school. Others recall to what degree their teacher preparation program actually prepared them for their current classroom. Many confess a sense of loss, lamenting over the one student who "got away" or longing for a return to teaching and learning as it once was, with the rewards written directly on the faces of the kids in the classroom, not on a pie chart or bar graph of how many grades meet or exceed the standards on an annual test. Yet several teachers admit a sense of regret that grew out of the awareness that either teaching wasn't what they had imagined it to be or that they had not become the teachers they dreamed they would become.

My call for teachers to write an essay about the pressures of teaching was met with many tentative responses, as if to ask, *is my idea good enough?* or *is what I'm feeling worth talking about?* Often our emails back and forth would eventually free the idea, the pressure, from a place of hurt, anger, or disappointment in my colleague. Loss resonated throughout. Whether it was the loss of innocence during the first year of teaching, a student who could not be reached, or the system's behavior, I found myself responding "*Write it!*" I was reminded of the last line of one of my favorite poems, "One Art" by Elizabeth Bishop. ".... It's evident / the art of losing's not too hard to master / though it may look like (*Write it!*) a disaster."

My former eighth graders will tell you as much the next time you see them at the mall.

—Maureen Picard Robins

THE WITCH TRICK:

BECOMING MORE THAN
A ONE-TRICK PONY

Tim Clifford

Ms. HUGHES WAS a great disciplinarian. Everyone said so, including the principal who hired me for my first teaching job. That was why, my principal explained, he was going to partner me with Ms. Hughes. By observing her, I would learn to be a good teacher.

I was truly grateful. I had no teaching experience— not even student teaching. The vivid memories of my own middle school years, filled with paper projectiles and wedgies, had come back to haunt me. I awaited Ms. Hughes's arrival at the back of the classroom, watching paper planes zigzag languidly through the air.

An occasional spitball would splat on someone's neck, eliciting words I hadn't learned in the entire course of my own middle school education. How anyone could tame these feral beasts, otherwise known as eighth graders, was beyond my comprehension.

Eventually, the brass doorknob turned and Ms. Hughes strode into the room. The classroom fell motionless, as if someone had turned off all the adolescent energy with a switch. The students sat silently and stared straight ahead. Some clasped their hands on the desk in from of them, elementary school-style, looking attentive. Even I sat up a bit straighter. There was no doubt about it—Ms. Hughes had a presence. She was tall, big-boned, and wore clothes that barely contained her mass. Her hair was neat but frizzy, as if hairspray could hardly contain it. Yet, as physically intimidating as she was, it was nothing compared to her sharp, gravelly voice.

"I see paper on the floor," she scowled. "Who threw it?"

Dead silence.

"All right, it seems as though we've forgotten," continued Ms. Hughes with the exaggerated sarcasm of a drill sergeant addressing recalcitrant recruits. "Let me hear it, ten times."

On cue, the class stood up in practiced unison and chanted, "Ms. Hughes is a witch! Ms. Hughes is a witch! Ms. Hughes..." They continued on in their loud sharp cadence until they reached their tenth repetition.

Then they sat as one, hands clasped once more, in a vacuum of silence.

"Very good," intoned Ms. Hughes. "Today, we're going to learn about the Pythagorean theorem."

I have no idea how long I sat there with my mouth hanging open. It was clear to me that to be considered a "good teacher" I'd have to be able to maintain the same iron-fisted control over my classes as Ms. Hughes had. As the school year progressed, however, the cracks in her approach began to show. The witch trick didn't work quite as well by Christmas, and her voice got louder and shriller with each passing month. By the time June arrived, no amount of hairspray could have kept Ms. Hughes's locks in place. She looked as if she'd been through the wringer because, in fact, she had. She was a one-trick pony.

That was 20 years ago, and such tactics might be considered abusive today. The definition of a good teacher has morphed somewhat since then, as well. While the best teachers always maintain discipline, it doesn't follow that the best disciplinarians are always good teachers. Moreover, while all teachers have at least a little Ms. Hughes in them, we need a few more tricks in our bags than she had.

Not only is every class different, but every child is different, so I won't be so bold as to propose a one-size-fits-all remedy for handling discipline problems. Sometimes you must form an uneasy alliance with children, especially the ones with the most stubborn behavioral problems. This often involves ceding some of your power in exchange for peace. Nevertheless, if learning takes place then in the end, you have done your job.

Therefore, I present to you five behavior archetypes, along with some suggestions for dealing with them.

ARCHETYPE #1: THE VOLCANO

Children come to us with all sorts of issues, and anger sometimes lurks just below the surface, waiting to erupt. One such child I remember vividly was Tatiana. She lived with her mother and two uncles, both of whom were prominent members of a local street gang. Simply put, education was the least of her problems. Luckily for me, she had a dead giveaway—when anger was getting the better of her, she would bounce her left leg up and down. When she was bouncing, I knew to watch out. The rest of the time, she could be polite, smart, and even engagingly funny. We developed that uneasy alliance; I would let her bounce when she needed to, but on her good days she had to do as I said.

Half way through the year, her good days far outnumbered her bad ones, and I nominated her for Student of the Month. The powers that be, who suspended Tatiana on a regular basis, were none too thrilled. They came to observe her one day, and I noted that her leg was bouncing furiously. I wanted to warn her observers, but they were faster than I was. One of them—who fancied herself a Ms. Hughes type, I think—immediately insisted that Tatiana throw out her gum. Tatiana coolly removed the gum, dropped the F-bomb, put the gum back in her mouth, and cracked it so loud that it could be heard in adjoining counties.

Tatiana was given a five-day in-school suspension on the spot, but she asked if she could still come to my class. It was fine by me. I knew the bounce trick.

When you run into your own Volcano, know the warning signs of an impending eruption. There are almost always tremors before the explosion, and if you can recognize them, you can usually avert catastrophe.

Archetype #2: The Wanderer

Wanderers are students whose object in life is to meander around, and sometimes leave, the classroom. There are many subclasses of the Wanderer: the Nose Blower (who always needs a tissue), the Pencil Sharpener, the Note Passer, and the Basket Shooter, to name but a few. These four types are mostly innocuous, as they tend to return to their seats within a minute. More troublesome are the Nurse's Sidekick, the Shrunken Bladder, and the Guidance Counselor's Pet. These hardcore Wanderers spend most of their school day plotting ways to get out of the classroom and stay out. Regardless of the subclass, the main goal of a Wanderer to be somewhere, *anywhere,* but at his or her seat.

Sometimes dealing with a Wanderer means setting rules for the whole class that you'd rather not set. For example, you may need to mandate a specific time to clear desks of debris to keep the Basket Shooter in check. For the Nose Blower, ask parents to buy individual size tissue packs for their children. Students who like to leave the class are harder to deal with. If a Shrunken Bladder says he has to go but you think he's faking, you'd better be right or there will be hell to pay from the parent who has to come to school with fresh underwear.

I recently had a student who seemed to be all types of the Wanderer rolled into one very mobile package. On any given day, this child could claim to be sick, in need of guidance, and have dull pencils all at the same time. Almost in desperation, I purchased a roll of tickets such as you'd see at a carnival. I gave each student three tickets and told the class each ticket was a free pass out of my room. They could use it to go wherever they wanted and whenever they needed to, but they had to have a ticket to leave. Once they were out of tickets, they were out of luck. Of course, I couldn't really enforce that, because sometimes you just gotta go, ticket or no ticket. However, the students didn't know that. I thought the plan would be a failure when the Wanderer used two of his tickets in the first two days. Then I had a brainstorm. I put the other half of everyone's tickets into a jar and held a raffle. Students who still had tickets could win valuable prizes, such as erasers shaped like dogs.

You'd have thought the prize was a million dollars the way the Wanderer held on to his final ticket. He didn't leave the room for a month. In a way, I felt that I was rewarding children just for doing what they were supposed to do, but I couldn't deny that it worked. I got more teaching done with fewer interruptions, and the Wanderer eventually won a dog eraser. That's what I like to think of as a win-win situation.

ARCHETYPE #3: THE BEAN SPILLER

Teachers generally hate to dampen enthusiasm, so Bean Spillers are often hard for us to deal with. Bean Spillers are the students who know—or think they know—the answers to every question and will do anything to be called on. They may rocket out of their chairs with their hands up, make sounds indicative of intestinal distress, or simply blurt out answers before anyone else has a chance to. The worst part is that we frequently help create these behavioral Frankensteins by giving in and asking for their response. Most teachers, including me, hate a prolonged silence, so the Bean Spiller can seem, at times, to be our best friend.

The solution is simple enough in most cases: call on other students. While this is easier said than done, it is usually quite effective. The Blurter, however, is the most stubborn of the Bean Spillers and will call out the answers no matter how much we may wish to ignore him or her. A recent Blurter of mine, Nathaniel, is a case in point.

He is a nice enough child but has difficulties controlling himself. I decided to try a variation of a turn and talk strategy with him. I paired him with a shy student—an anti-Bean Spiller, if you will. I asked them to discuss a story, and report what the other person had said about it. This effectively put the brakes on Nathaniel; he was willing to discuss what his partner had said, but wasn't jumping out of his seat about it. His partner, who was normally reluctant to speak, seemed more willing to participate now that it wasn't his own answer he was presenting.

This worked on two levels: it helped me dampen Nathaniel's constant desire to give the answer, and it helped the shy student participate with less risk. It's not perfect, of course. I can't use this technique on every question, every day. Still, it addressed the weakness of each student, and allowed others in the class to get a word in edgewise. Finally.

ARCHETYPE #4: THE GENERAL

I met Vicky during my first weeks of teaching. By any standard you'd care to name, she was a tough cookie. Vicky was smart enough to recognize that I had a tenuous grip on classroom discipline, so she decided to become a General. She had a loud voice and a menacing look. All the students in the class were scared of her. Truth be told, I was a little scared of her myself. It was clear that if she had ordered her classmates to attack me, they would have. She even had her own lieutenant, a tiny boy named Luis. Whatever Vicky commanded, Luis would repeat.

"Hey, Mr. Clifford," Vicky would say. "I think we should all get to talk for the last ten minutes of class today."

"Yeah! We should talk like Vicky said!" echoed Luis.

And so they talked.

It was ridiculous. When Vicky told the class to talk, they would talk. When she told them to shut up (a phrase to which she was much addicted), they would. No one wanted to cross her, least of all me. I decided that I would either have to find a way to work with her or lose my mind. One day, I decided to give out classroom jobs, and I asked Vicky to be my assistant.

"Assistant?" she asked suspiciously.

"What do you mean, assistant?" said Luis, backing her up.

"This is a tough class," I said. "I need a helper to write names down on the board when someone misbehaves."

"You want me to boss around my classmates?" she said, amazed that someone wanted her to do officially what she had done voluntarily all her life.

"Not boss. Just help me decide who's doing the right thing and the wrong thing."

She almost ripped the piece of chalk from my hand. "You hear that?" she bellowed, addressing the class. "Mr. Clifford made me his assistant! God help you if I write your name on the board!"

"Say your prayers!" intoned Luis.

Not surprisingly, few names had to be written on the board for the rest of the year. Vicky was thrilled to have a teacher who viewed her not as a nuisance, but as a blessing. She was a great General. Sometimes you have to figure out a way to use a student's gifts to your own advantage.

Archetype #5: The Elevator Operator

Perhaps the most common species of classroom behavior problem is the Elevator Operator. We've all had plenty of them. They know just what buttons to press to drive you crazy.

My most recent Elevator Operator was Eugene. He was the most vexing type of Operator, the passive-aggressive. He would never do anything outlandish to get himself in trouble; in fact, he seemed perfectly content to lay back and deliver a zinger with the innocence of a newborn child. One of his favorite tactics was to ask for clarification of whatever it was I had just said.

"Okay, class," I would say. "Let's take out our reader's notebooks and write a response to what we've just read."

"Mr. Clifford," Eugene would say. "Do you want us to take out our reader's notebook or writer's notebook?"

"Reader's."

"And put them on the desk?"

"Yes."

"Then what do we do?"

"Write a response to what we just read."

"In our reader's or writer's notebook?"

I'm convinced that Elevator Operators are in it just for the attention. They're not slow or inattentive—in fact, they probably pay more attention than 90 percent of students, or else they couldn't ask the maddeningly pointless questions that they do. They just love watching their teacher's blood pressure skyrocket as they hit each successive button.

The only way to deal with an Elevator Operator is to stop responding to the button pushes. It's difficult, I know, because as teachers, we are trained to respond to the needs of students. Moreover, the Elevator Operator, having failed to get a response, will push harder and faster for a time. Nevertheless, if you stick with it, eventually he or she will give up and take the stairs.

I know that Ms. Hughes would disapprove of much of this essay and with many of the techniques I've used. Still, one thing I have learned over the years is that a class is comprised of many individuals with many different traits and needs, and no one solution works for everyone or every situation. Some students will cooperate with everything you try to do, but others will force you to forge that uneasy alliance, that fine line between your way and the highway. In the end, I've found that creativity works better than Ms. Hughes's brute force— and as a bonus, you'll end up using less hairspray.

VENGLISH

Bryan Ripley Crandall

I N 1998, DURING my first year as a classroom teacher, I encountered an unexpected change in pedagogy. Whereas the demographics at the school that hired me had been about 50 percent African American and 50 percent Caucasian up until then, the school began enrolling an influx of Vietnamese students. My freshman English classes were to be a room of 8 Vietnamese students, 10 African American students, and 12 Caucasian students. I was already nervous about memorizing new names, but now I had to fear not being able to pronounce the names, too. The monosyllabic sounds of Vietnamese titles were unfamiliar to my name repertoire—and we were unaccustomed to the renaissance of bilingual students arriving at our school. We didn't have an English as a second language (ESL) program, nor had anyone predicted the population changes our city was experiencing. As a result, I gained a palate for "Venglish"—the fusion of Vietnamese and English—early in my teaching career. Our urban community, as well as our understanding of human experience, was beautifully enriched through such powerful, new communities.

By the second year of this population shift, school administrators recognized our need for ESL support. Teachers grew perplexed about assessing Vietnamese students and shared concern about spoken communication. Several began looking for texts written by Vietnamese writers, only to learn their generation of immigrant stories was so new that, such books had not yet been written. Our district had ESL resources at other schools, however, and they were able to tap into the growing pool of knowledgeable ESL teachers in our district. They suggested we hire a man already known to Vietnamese students. This ESL teacher seamlessly integrated his perspectives into our already diverse culture by assisting all classroom instruction. After two years with us, however, his wife took employment out of state and he had to move. With growing ESL populations in every school, replacing his expertise was difficult. There were not enough ESL educators available.

For this reason, our administration created a teaching space for me to work one hour a day with our Vietnamese students. Uncertified and lacking knowledge for working with English language learners, I quickly gained insight from the frustration of living in a second language, especially while teaching American subjects rich with content, equations, and lectures. Helping the Vietnamese students get through fast-paced chapters of American history, working with biology teachers to make vocabulary accessible to ESL learners, and finding ways to break F. Scott Fitzgerald's *The Great Gatsby* into digestible chunks became a Gordian knot to unravel in only one hour every day.

This hour of ESL instruction quickly turned into 60 minutes of Venglish. Their conversations in Vietnamese outnumbered our English ones, as they naturally spoke their home language, gossiping with each other about my quirky sense of humor and their personal lives. Some students had between five and eight years of American schooling already. Two young ladies had less than a year. Even so, their task was to become better communicators in a new land, and they each understood the importance of becoming better speakers of the English language. We debated whether my "ESL class" should be an English-only zone or a fusion between both: Venglish was the result.

Our original ESL instructor lobbied hard with our admissions committee to create strong ties with the city's growing English language learner (ELL) community and wished our school to become a home for many immigrant students. Because our school had a pre-existing mission of diversity and individuality, he saw it as a natural, multicultural fit. As our city changed, he argued, so should the representation of diverse cultures at our school. The opposition to his lobbying came from those who feared the effect it would have on test scores. Bringing in ELL students prompted conversations about culture that made teachers nervous—our dialogue on diversity had previously been one based on black and white binaries. Adding a new, more global perspective instigated new thinking about the ways we teachers "did school." Some complained they already had too much to do.

Even so, my Vietnamese students and I bonded to get at the complicated, difficult curriculum as best we could. From such mentoring, it was inevitable that personal stories arrived to challenge my role as an educator. The original ESL teacher did successfully promoted several applicants applying for our school. One of these applicants was a young man named Bao Lanh (a pseudonym). The ESL teacher told us Bao was a struggling student who had an enormous heart and would benefit from the receptive warmth of our school. He was known to crawl into the laps of his teachers while they read stories to students, and to look attentively at lips while they offered new American words. I first met Bao when his English teacher noted he was the only student in our new freshman class who didn't get permission to spend the night during a team-building, camping experience. The ESL teacher asked if I would drive him each day to be with his classmates, which I did. When the ESL teacher moved to another state, though, Bao was assigned to my makeshift ESL class. He was an attentive, curious, and hardworking student.

At his going-away party, the ESL teacher asked me to pay special attention to Bao. He said Bao's life was atypical and he needed a lot of mentoring and support. He made me promise I'd be an advocate. Bao, I was told, lived with his uncle in community housing offered to new immigrants. Their relationship was extremely strained. It was believed Bao's mother was still in Vietnam and speculated she did not live a desirable life. When the chance arrived, she sent Bao to America to have a "better" life. Bao met relatives already resettled in our city, and these aunts and uncles decided it was best for Bao to live in a two-bedroom apartment with an aging, needy uncle. As an elementary school student, Bao would care for their uncle and help him around his apartment.

Midway through his sophomore year, after our loss of ESL support, Bao had an altercation with a classmate. This fight became the catalyst for my understanding of Bao's complicated world. Another boy was making fun of Bao's being Asian, and Bao snapped. He jumped the boy and did serious damage to the kid's eye. Although the other boy was known as a verbal punk within the school, administrators suspended Bao (as they should have). When it came time for Bao's return, however, school leaders were skeptical and wanted to send him to an alternative school. The outburst seemed too violent and Bao's reliability as a safe student was put into question. Hearing the ESL teacher's request in the back of my mind, I went to battle for Bao and convinced the administration he deserved a second chance—which he got.

As a result, Bao Lanh began hanging out in my classroom, calling me at my home, and hovering around me whenever he could. From this proximity, I began noticing many lacerations on his arm—and having had cutters in class before, I directly addressed his wounds. A good friend of mine, an adolescent psychologist, often talked with me about why some students break their skin. Cutting, I was told, is an act of "feeling alive" when a person "feels dead inside." I used this knowledge to understand Bao better. His self-mutilation was a reminder that he was trying to feel, but it also helped me to realize there was something wrong. I arranged for Bao to meet my psychologist friend, but Bao declined. He promised, instead, to let me know when he was about to cut, but reassured me that he "had it under control." Such bravado was par for Bao's course and I made a decision to keep my school's counselor informed about what I knew.

There was a night in February of that year, though, when the doorway of our relationship opened slightly more. It was freezing outside and Bao called to tell me he was in a very dark place. His uncle had locked him in his bedroom—a punishment—and Bao began sticking his hands out his window into the ice-cold air until they were frozen. He then brought them inside and cracked his fingers, mesmerized by their bleeding. He wouldn't say why he was doing this, but wanted me to know he was, indeed, hurting himself. He reported he had a knife with him, as well. I did whatever mentoring I knew how to do, and asked questions while trying to get him to talk. This seemed to calm him down, and I made him promise he would tell me about why he felt the need to create such harm on himself. He came the next day.

Several Vietnamese youth in the community became victims of poverty, Americanization, and adolescent frustration. Local news reported the rise of Vietnamese gang activity, and at age 15, Bao Lanh was dabbling in this territory. A police officer told me the Vietnamese gangs were becoming the worst in the city. Bao also revealed that his uncle was crazy and abusive. In fact, as a young boy, Bao said he was sometimes tied to his bed at night with metal chains pulled so tight they created bruises on his chest and legs. Teachers at his elementary school contacted authorities because the marks were obvious. Social workers were called, yet perhaps because of the language barrier, nothing resulted. Bao felt tortured in his own apartment, and he therefore became more self-abusive.

As Bao's body and strength grew, he knew he could cause physical harm to his uncle, but chose instead to cut himself and to run the streets with friends who made him feel tough. Bao was bulky and muscular for his age, and he prided himself on appearing "thick." He took his

aggravation and turned it toward the thrill of drugs, dis-
obedience, and drinking. Older boys in the community
who had dropped out of school offered him structural
support by encouraging his recklessness. A disregard
for laws was already prevalent in his housing development, too: the ice cream truck, he admitted, worked as
a cover for selling cigarettes, pornography, and weap-
ons to young kids. He reported being shot at, beaten by
other gangs, and left sick on the streets from partying,
but it was still better, he claimed, than dealing with his
"senile" uncle.

I adhered to what any teacher should do, I went
directly to the counselor at my school to make a report.
She advised me to call protective agencies, which I did.
Making the call was hard, but the social service agencies
were well aware of Bao's situation. That is as much as
they would tell me. There was a history I would never
know, and caseworkers were very involved.

The first year, Bao did well at our school, but soon
after his fight in the sophomore year, he became more
and more truant. Life on the streets gained more promi-
nence in his life. I still called him often, but I felt that he
was slipping away.

Knowing it was a matter of time until he gave up
completely, I invited an aunt, the uncle, and Bao out
to lunch to show my concern, acknowledge his success
at our school, and declare his immense potential as an
American student. I wanted to present Bao in a positive

light to his family, and to ask them to help me keep him in school. The meeting didn't go as planned, though. The uncle grew very angry. The aunt translated that Bao was a hassle to the uncle, and caused much grief to the family. She said that Bao's uncle felt he needed a good beating, that Bao was a "terrible kid." I asked Bao why his uncle punched his arms and chest while speaking, and Bao told me his uncle was declaring how he thought American teachers and schools were weak. He blamed American schools for Bao's terrible behavior, but this is not what the aunt had translated. Bao sighed. "Now you see how he sees me. I don't have a father. I don't have a mother. I have this."

Soon after this lunch meeting, Bao Lanh stopped attending school. He failed his classes. His Vietnamese classmates began educating me with more of Bao's history, including how his cousins also attended our school, which I hadn't known. I talked immediately with them and other classmates about Bao's whereabouts, and all they would tell me was that he was a choosing a bad life and his uncle was a crazy man. His cousins were college-bound achievers who seemed to express immense frustration with their relative who didn't live by the same code of ethics.

In the fall of the next year, Bao still came by to see me, although he had relocated to another school. Administrators suspected he came into our school to sell drugs, and he was quickly escorted away each time. There was a day, though, when he successfully found his way to my room and, knowing how the administration would view it, I told him to visit me at home or to call me, but that coming to our school was not smart at all. Our school was off-limits—which is ironic because for kids like him, school is often the only safe place they have. I contacted teachers at Bao's new school and asked them to keep an eye on him. But like many of the other students who attend my school, he stopped attending.

The spring of that same year I received a letter from a youth retention center outside our city. It requested that I become an advocate for Bao Lanh, by corresponding with him while he was held in a progressive military program/GED prep course. Bao had given the authorities my name. I didn't know why he was there, but signed on to be his mentor. His letters were usually about how he was feeling, how thankful he was I still believed in him, and how he would return a changed man. His classmates repeated rumors that Bao had snapped and finally pulled a gun on his uncle, and that he had been arrested and taken to this juvenile facility. There, he finished course work successfully, and I was sent a note that praised Bao's high marks and remarked that he had successfully completed his GED as one of the best students. I awaited the promise from Bao that he would use this opportunity to change his life.

That promise, however, never arrived. Instead, I didn't hear from Bao Lanh for almost a year. One day his good friend stopped by my school to inquire if I would accept a call from Bao. I was told Bao was "on the run," but I wasn't told why. It was 3:00 AM on a school night when the phone rang. The caller ID showed an out-of-state number. I answered and talked with Bao Lanh for an hour in my last attempt to piece together his puzzle. He told me that after he left the detention school, he fell back into the street life and trouble with the law. If he returned to our state, Bao said, he'd be arrested for a very long time. I quickly had to think about the best action to take—and I chose honesty. I asked him not to contact me until he was sure he was ready to begin healing, which included turning himself into authorities and seeking help. I told him I still believed in him with all my soul and that it was painful for me to believe in him more than he believed in himself. A lot went through my head. *Had I done everything I could? Was I partly responsible for assisting a kid wanted by the law? Were the stories he told me about his life true? How does one save a kid like Bao?* We hung up the phone that night with a promise he'd contact me soon and that it was his mission not to disappoint me.

I still think of Bao in the way he was introduced to me by the original ESL teacher. I see him as a good kid who sought shelter from a bad life. When I agreed to try my luck for one hour a day as a temporary ESL instructor at my school, I didn't know how much the personal lives of these students would affect my understanding of

American schools. Working with all the Vietnamese students offered greater depth to my understanding of global issues and to my knowledge about the difficulty of immigrating to our American culture, and in the complicated lifework that occurs for these students in and outside of school. As educators make curriculum more and more rigorous to meet the demands of political expectations, we also add greater frustration for the populations who are marginalized the most by traditional educational contexts and teachers. Students learn best from strong, personal ties with their schools and teachers, yet such relationships are not the best preparation for multiple-choice exams and national assessments.

Perhaps this is why I hope to hear from Bao Lanh, again one day, as he promised. When he contacts me, I imagine him telling me about his struggle since we last talked and how he kept our conversations close to his heart, body, and soul. In this scenario, I imagine Bao telling me about how his son and daughter climb into his lap every night as he reads them their favorite stories. He says he loves looking into their eyes and giving them the childhood he never knew. I have to believe this is the way the story ends.

The Pressures of Teaching Special Education

Chrissy Corbisiero

Let me break it down for you, so you
know what I say is true:
I make a goddamn difference! What about you?
"What do I make? I make a goddamn
difference. What about you?"

—Taylor Mali

WHILE THE PRESSURES of teaching cannot be described accurately in an essay or even a book, I must preface this piece by saying that it is precisely these pressures and challenges that make teaching one of the most valuable, worthwhile professions in the world. I have held jobs in various industries, and being a special education teacher is the most difficult, yet most rewarding, thing I have ever done. Ironically, in an attempt to teach young minds with specific disabilities, I have learned more about myself than I ever expected. It is through this journey of self-discovery that I found my true calling and the most sincere form of happiness.

I taught special education in a self-contained environment for five years. In the world of special education, a self-contained environment is one of the most restrictive settings for students with disabilities. These classes serve students with the greatest need for educational services. There are only 12 students to one teacher, who is sometimes supported by a paraprofessional (or classroom assistant). The students with whom I have worked have displayed a wide range of disabilities. Autism, mental retardation, emotional disturbance, traumatic brain injury, multiple disabilities, cerebral palsy, and general learning disabilities are just some of the names given to the obstacles my students face on a daily basis. These official diagnoses, however, do not encompass the full multitude of both physical and emotional hardships that accompany these disabilities.

In speaking to my peers, who have jobs that follow a standard corporate-America, nine-to-five path, the goings-on of my classroom usually elicit a response of disbelief, laughter, or even pity, sometimes accompanied by a "why in the world are you doing this?" sort of look. Over time, I have come to prepare myself, usually by exhibiting a stoic lack of response to any one of these reactions when I tell a story in passing. People always want to hear more about my "crazy students" and what their latest antics are. When I first started sharing stories of children throwing desks, attacking teachers, flipping tables, and not being able to spell their first names, it was more because I couldn't believe what I was seeing, not because I wanted to pawn off my class as the next cast for *Dangerous Minds*. Initially, I didn't quite comprehend that these behaviors were the direct result of their disabilities and didn't know why they were in my class to begin with.

Even now, at times I regret mentioning things that have occurred in my classroom, resenting the sort of fascination these stories elicit, fascination usually reserved for circus freaks. What I'd like to say (*Please shut up and stop laughing at my students!*) and what I typically reply (*Yup,* with a quiet, friendly smile) are usually not the same, which brings me to one of the special "pressures" associated with special education: the disconnect from not only the general population, but from others within the field of education.

The feeling of isolation that is so common in special education for both students and teachers can be discouraging. With students often placed in a separate wing of the school, the physical isolation of special education programs can set the tone for the social separation that follows. In a self-contained environment, students rarely interact with the general population, and come to live in an impenetrable bubble of sorts. Students are often ridiculed for being "special," and there are few ways to camouflage these differences, particularly when their separateness is accentuated in so many different ways. Separate classes. Separate teachers. Separate buses. Separate lunch tables. Being labeled as a special education student can be downright embarrassing for many students, which, in combination with an existing disability, can make a child's school experience that much more difficult.

This sense of apartheid that exists for special education students, while almost startling at first, becomes almost invisible as time goes on. I cannot tell you how many times my students have been left out of school-wide activities. During my first year of teaching, my self-contained students were not given schedules to follow on the first day of school, already a traumatizing experience for most youths. As the rest of the general education students clung to their schedules and referred to them as maps to some hidden treasure, my students wandered aimlessly around, waiting for someone to tell them where to go. I was disappointed to see that this was only the beginning of how differently my "special" students were treated. From the most mundane occurrences (being called for lunch) to the most significant school events (graduation, honor roll, and even fire drills), my students were simply deleted—sometimes by accident, sometimes not.

Unfortunately, as time went on, I began to accept this as one of the many injustices that came with being "separate but equal." What still disturbed me, though, was that this learned helplessness had become almost innate for my students by the time they reached middle school, and that this concept was often heavily reinforced by my students' families. I came to see that so many of them had not experienced typical, regular life experiences, and it was hard to determine where this cycle began. One student, Maria, had never been allowed to play with her peers outside of school because her mother was too nervous for her safety. Another student, Sara, had never been food shopping and was amazed at the wonders of the grocery store. John had never been to the public library, and it actually brought tears to my eyes to see how happy he was to be around so many books. It was only after exposing my students to these seemingly ordinary life experiences that I wondered about the origin of this separateness. What came first, the chicken or the egg?

With each student came a distinct set of emotions and events, which led me to see that students could react very differently to being placed in a self-contained environment. Some were really in denial of the fact that they were in special education. I remember a student, James, for example, who would repeatedly call everyone else in the class "retarded" (myself included) while ranting about how he was put in the class by mistake. On average, he used the word about 50 times a day. He claimed it was just a matter of time before his mom got the situation straightened out. He hurt others because he felt he was being punished, and the verbal attacks were only the beginning of his defiance.

On the other hand, leaving the isolated world of special education is not every kid's dream. Some students actually took comfort in the fact that they were in their own small world, sometimes to an excessive point in which they became fearful of general education and the big wide world outside their classroom door. When Michael was doing quite well in our class of 12 students, I thought he would be excited to try mainstream classes. He trembled at the thought, and after months of coaxing him into it, finally agreed to give it a shot. Needless to say, Michael didn't do well, and returned to my small class in a matter of days. He complained of too many kids, a lack of attention, and loud noises. He did not comment, however, on his reprieve from segregation from the masses.

This feeling of isolation associated with special education is not limited to just students; it usually also extends to teachers both within and outside of the classroom. Because middle schools and high schools are so heavily divided by subject area, special education teachers can struggle when it comes to gathering materials for specific classes. We are expected to be renaissance men and women, jacks of all trades, if you will, teaching all levels and content areas. I taught sixth grade English, sixth grade social studies, and eighth grade math simultaneously. I didn't necessarily mind the diversity of the instruction—it was more the preparation that caused me stress. I often felt "homeless" when it was time for content area meetings which, provided teachers with helpful ideas on what to do and teach. While I highly valued all of the things that I learned in each content area, I remember constantly wondering what I was missing in the other meetings, and whether I was somehow doing a disservice to my students. To compensate for this, I constantly asked for help from other teachers and administrators. Some were more than willing to provide me with materials and insight, for which I was enormously grateful. Others were not as gracious. I remember a senior teacher looking absolutely dumbfounded when I mentioned that I needed textbooks for my special education classes. She said, "Oh. I don't have anything for them." And that was that. Accommodating the needs of my special education students was not exactly high on the list of others' priorities. That was my job.

Outside of the classroom, my teaching experiences became a form of entertainment for my family and friends. As I mentioned earlier, they begged me for stories, which I initially mistook for interest. After a while, I became reluctant to share stories of my students'

struggles because they were met with laughter or ridi-
cule. The truth of the matter was, with summers off and
being done by three o'clock during the school year, non-
teachers thought I was walking on Easy Street. They
didn't (and couldn't) understand the daily rigor of being
a teacher, and a special education one at that. I poured
every ounce of my heart and soul into my students, and
this was something that no outsider could comprehend.
I felt alone.

My first year of teaching was probably the most
intense, in terms of isolation. How could I explain to
someone that Anthony had thrown his desk across the
room, but that I was still willing to help him? How could
I tell my parents that Julia had tried to slit her wrists in
my classroom, but I was the only one she would talk to?
Could I really convey the depth of emotions that were
displayed in my room on a daily basis to someone who
had not witnessed it firsthand?

People told me to quit. They told me I hadn't gradu-
ated from an Ivy League school only to get cursed out on
a daily basis. I got tired of having to explain why I was
sticking with it, and why quitting was never an option
that crossed my mind. I understood my role as a teacher,
and ironically through this sort of isolation from the outside world, I came to see my classroom as one of the few
places I really felt that I belonged. Explaining the intensity of this emotional roller coaster to those who viewed

work as a nine-to-five time killer was just not something I felt was necessary. Therefore, I held it in.

In addition to this, the other all-encompassing pressure that is perhaps more significant in special education than other areas is classroom management. As I considered this next obstacle, I began to wonder what classroom management really meant to those outside the field of education. I actually asked a few of my friends what came to mind when I said this term. Some said it conjured up an image of a classroom neatly aligned in rows. Others said they thought it meant how a classroom is run (as in what procedures the teacher required—hanging up coats, etc.). One answer stuck out in my mind: one of my friends simply said, "It's everything the teacher needs to do in order to teach." I found this to be particularly insightful and accurate because in my opinion, classroom management refers to a broad range of responsibilities on both the part of the teacher and the students. Effective classroom management is not only important, but also essential. In other words, if a teacher doesn't have control of his or her classroom, nothing gets done. Period.

Classroom management is a struggle for many new teachers, and remains a challenge even for the seasoned ones. It's something that mostly comes with experience, and also depends heavily on the nature of the students in the class and the teacher as a person. What works with one group may flop with another. It's about finding a balance that not only allows each student to stay afloat, but also allows him or her to function at a level that is both appropriate and challenging at the same time.

When working with students whose difficult behavior is second nature (usually a direct result of their disability), it is especially hard to maintain consistency, and sometimes sanity, on a daily basis. However, it is consistency that is the key to establishing any sort of control. The things that I have seen as a special educator in New York City schools are worthy of an entire book, which I hope to complete one day. Nevertheless, for now, I will limit my list to the things that most seriously influenced my classroom management system. Loud noises, wildly inappropriate language, physical fights (also being physically attacked), chairs and desks being thrown across a room, and "runners" (students who regularly run out of the classroom) are just a taste of the things to be addressed under the umbrella of classroom management in a self-contained special education classroom. No one can imagine all of the minutiae involved in combating even just one of these issues. No matter how much I would prepare, it was a certainty that I would be caught off-guard at some point by something my students did or said.

In order to avoid this, I made sure that my classroom management plan encompassed not only behavior modifications, but also a positive academic environment. In some classes, I had students who performed at a kindergarten level in the same class as those on a fifth-grade equivalent. Academic issues aside, one of my biggest challenges was creating an open emotional atmosphere in which each student could do well without feeling dumb or out of place. I tackled this by constantly referring to the class as a family, which included me in a sort of parental role. I tried, in every way possible, to operate under this attitude, which I think helped to create a sense of unity within the room. While I remained fairly open, it was also clear who was in charge and deserved respect.

This approach helped when it came to disagreements among students. While we did not always see eye to eye, we were all on the same team and therefore needed to settle our differences. This was actually one of the times when the isolation came in handy. For example, there came a time when calling in the "authorities" (crisis teams, security, deans, or administrators) became an insignificant consequence to some of the students. They knew the drill: misbehave, someone gets called, they get removed from class, a minor punishment, then back to class as usual. When I stressed that we would have to solve a problem ourselves without resorting to outside interference (suspensions and the like), students were surprised and became more willing to compromise. They seemed happier to be respected enough to solve their own problems. While this was by no means a quick fix to all of the chaos in the classroom, I do believe that it built a foundation of respect from which everyone benefited.

However, it is only with a united approach that successful classroom management can be properly executed. This being said, the third pressure that can really make or break a teacher's success is the relationship between the administration (the people who run the school) and the teachers. While I would never think to undermine the difference that an individual teacher can make, if the administrators and the teachers are not on the same page, then chaos can, and most likely will, occur. Simply stated, teachers can only do so much. It was only after working for an amazing school that I came to see what a difference this made in the lives of both the teachers and the students. The policies and procedures of a school affect everything from behavior to academic performance.

If a school's administration ignores bad behavior, then there are few things a teacher can threaten a student with. For example, during my very first week of teaching, I was physically assaulted by a high school student. My assistant principal told me that I would "get used to it." From then on, the student knew that she wouldn't be punished for anything and her behavior continued to spiral out of control. Needless to say, it was a tough year in which I had to rack my brain for sources of motivation just to survive. Chaos was an understatement, and I had no one to back me up.

The administration's standard for academic success also sets the tone for the entire school. If students know that no one other than their teacher is taking responsibility for their performance, they will be a lot less inclined to try their hardest. When it is clear that education and academics are a school wide priority, then students are going to raise the bar for themselves. This also gives teachers more incentive to ensure that their students are performing appropriately. On the flipside, sometimes administrators can put an inordinate amount of pressure on their teachers, which becomes even more challenging when students' abilities are limited.

For teachers to teach effectively amidst all of these immense barriers is an enormous task sometimes met with little success. It is for this reason that any small change made in a student's life, even a seemingly insignificant one, is so meaningful.

The love and passion that is required of an effective teacher is not something that comes naturally to all people, and is certainly not something that can be given by just anyone. To me, it is one of the rawest forms of self-sacrifice, one that requires dedication and endurance. Moreover, while the difficulty has seemed unparalleled at times, there has been no greater experience in my life.

Stress by Censorship

Mary Ann Ellis

M Y STOMACH CHURNED as I walked into the boardroom and sat near the front. I chose a chair immediately behind my principal, Phil Murphy, and only a few feet from the four board members who were already seated. Mr. Barlow, the habitual latecomer, had not yet arrived. Mr. Ammons, board chairperson sat in the middle of the horseshoe-arranged tables, chatting with Dr. Webb, the tall, thin superintendent. Mrs. Tillman and Mrs. Carter, both retired teachers, interspersed their chatter with laughter. Their white hair hinted at wisdom. In spite of the veneer of amicability, the hostility in the room was palpable, thick, and deadly—deadly because of a couple of time-honored classics that had been taught indefinitely in Appling County, Georgia.

"We studied those books back when I was in high school here in the sixties," my husband Larry told me when he first heard of the controversy.

On June 11, 2007, Reverand Barry Teutsch, a local minister, dubbed these books pornography, and from that very day the school board leaned toward agreement. During his speech to the board, he said, "I've never read such foul and vulgar language as that in *Of Mice and Men*. The book also degrades the black race. Why, just yesterday in my pulpit, I preached against this very thing. A student showed me *Native Son* yesterday and it's even worse."

At board meetings he preached to the board, shouting down people who disagreed with him. "Reverand Teutsch, your time is up. You've been talking for 15 minutes," said Mr. Ammons.

"Well, do you want me to stop?" the minister inquired.

"Let him continue," several board members agreed, and he did—for another 15 minutes. They dared not close the mouth that spoke for God.

When I spoke to that same board in favor of education, classic literature, and our students—especially our Advanced Placement ones, the members were unimpressed. As chairperson of the English department, I was corrupting young minds—or so they thought.

For the past 23 years, I've been actively reading and writing with the best young minds of Appling County, training them for college. An avid reader myself, I have multiple degrees and have attended untold conferences and workshops to increase my teaching skills and knowledge. As a rule, my students do well when they leave to go to college. Proudly, they come back from UGA, GSU, Mercer, Emory, even Harvard to hang their successes on the walls of their alma mater. Eight STAR Teacher plaques hang on my walls, and I was named Systemwide Teacher of the Year in 1997. When Reverand Teutsch dubbed me a "so-called Christian," all my acclaim and expertise flew out the window. Suddenly, he became the person to select books for Appling County schools.

From June 11, 2007, through November of that year, I spent hours sitting in that second row seat in the boardroom. Every single time Reverand Teutsch rose to speak, my nerves tensed. During one meeting, he pointedly said, "Matthew 18:5 says, 'But whoso shall offend one of these little ones which believe in me, it were better for him that a millstone were hanged about his neck, and that he were drowned in the depth of the sea.'" He waved his Bible for emphasis as he spoke.

He preached a veritable sermon there in the boardroom with members of his congregation and a preacher friend in his amen corner. My stomach twisted anew with every word he said and with each nod of a board member. The atmosphere brought to mind an old-fashioned tent revival from my girlhood, not a board meeting.

Even though Reverand Teutsch insisted that his

reasons for condemning the books had nothing to do with religion, he found the books abhorrent because of the language that "took the Lord's name in vain" and violated our own discipline code. He pointed out the use of the word *nigger* in *Native Son* and insisted that our black students would be highly offended.

"Reverand Teutsch, did you know that Richard Wright, a black author, wrote *Native Son* as protest literature? He used this word strategically to make his point and even chose the name Bigger for his main character because it rhymes with *nigger* and would bring up the proper image in the reader's mind."

This literary critic, who had admittedly read neither book, blatantly ignored my explanation.

"When you force students to read foul language that you will not allow them to say," he stated emphatically, "you violate your own code in the ACHS handbook. You are forcing these students to take the Lord's name in vain."

He referred to our rule against the "use of profane, vulgar, or obscene words, gestures, or other actions." I suspect that every high school has such a rule. As a matter of fact, Principal Murphy pointed out to him that we teach our students about wars, too, but our handbook forbids violence.

Ironically enough, our policy has always been to provide alternate books for any student who objected or whose parents objected to the novels we read in class.

We'd never forced anyone to read a particular book. Reverand Teutsch found our policy inadequate as did the board of education, even though it had been in place for many years, more than the 23 of my teaching career in this county.

During the July 9 meeting, he asked, "When will the board remove these books? If they don't, then what is the protocol for removing teachers, principals, or even superintendents? I don't understand why you can't just teach all your literature directly from the Bible. Everything you could possibly need is right there."

As I sat listening, I slipped an antacid from its foil wrapper and into my mouth. My stomach was rolling, and my head was starting to throb.

A nonsupportive board and an accusing public ignorant of our purpose and methods brought inconceivable tension to my two colleagues and me, the three teachers of Honors English. We worried to the point of physical illness.

On the last day of summer vacation, July 31, the English department and Mr. Murphy met at school with Reverand Teutsch, his friend Reverand Brown, and one parent to explain and discuss our methods. Our superintendent had asked us to sit down and talk. We wasted our last tidbit of free time during the two hours we talked. Nothing we said changed his opinion one smidgen.

By this time, practically the whole community had taken sides. Vicious letters on both sides sold *The Baxley*

News-Banner. The owner of the local radio station also blasted the English department. He had not read the books either.

At a board meeting one night, he said to me, "Mrs. Ellis, I see no reason for reading fiction, period. It's a complete waste of time. That stuff's not even true."

How does one reply to such ignorance? I couldn't. I just stood there amazed.

In the meantime, school started and we teachers agonized over what to teach. My stomach pain was always there in the background, a sleeping monster, waiting for Reverand Teutsch to pounce again. My doctor had prescribed daily medication to keep the pain at bay, but neither she nor any pill could alleviate the stress. I was determined to continue teaching the books my students needed. After all, my first obligation is to them. The list of good books is so long that I could continue indefinitely, even if Reverand Teutsch brought regular complaints. The challengers didn't read the books I taught unless some student pointed out "bad" words to them, so I went about the business of teaching.

A tic in my eye came, unbidden, when any one mentioned the book situation, and it came up constantly. In Wal-Mart, supporters stopped me to talk about it and encourage me to stand against censorship. At school, other teachers encouraged me to continue the fight.

"What if he comes in here to direct the science curriculum?" a colleague asked. "It would be catastrophic."

"It could happen," I told her.

Truthfully, I do have a problem with Reverand Teutsch's attitude, but I have a worse problem with my school board's. I'm convinced that Reverand Teutsch truly believes what he's preaching, and he has no idea what we do in the English department to prepare our students for college. However, the five people who serve on the board of education were elected by the public to oversee and provide the best education possible for our students—all our students, not just the ones who plan to remain here in Baxley, Georgia, all their lives. Those students will not suffer for not having read the classics, but students who plan to major in English will.

Board members are not the experts, but they have access to those of us who are. Teachers are the trained professionals who know what students need to read to pass Advanced Placement exams and the SAT. We have studied the literary canon all our educational careers and longer. Instead of asking our opinions, the board took the word of the minister and removed these books from our classrooms. Students could check them out with parental permission, but we could not teach them in the classroom, even with 100 percent parental permission. This elected board not only stripped our students of their right to study these classics with a qualified teacher, it also stripped the parents of their rights.

At the insistence of the superintendent, the board did require Reverand Teutsch to follow the written procedure for challenging books in Appling County, but then ignored its own policy and overruled the recommendations of the two committees. Upon the original protest, the books went to the high school media committee made up of 14 people, including department heads and media specialists. This committee deemed the books appropriate for high school students and recommended they be kept in the curriculum.

Reverand Teutsch protested again. The books then went to the countywide media committee, made up of principals, media specialists, parents, and the curriculum director. This committee also recommended keeping the books, finding them completely appropriate for the grade level and content.

For three weeks after the formal complaint came, two committees of 20 respected educators *read* (a key word here) these two books, discussed them, and found them appropriate for high school students. Nonetheless, when the minister returned to the board, its members ignored the recommendation of the committees and voted unanimously to take the books out of the classroom. Many of the board members even refused to read the books.

Insidiously, into the controversy came another book, *Brave New World.* Reverand Teutsch added this classic to the list during a daytime meeting while I and most of the other literary education proponents were working. When he complained this time, he accused the board of dragging its feet, and subsequently goaded the members into voting. They removed the books from the classroom. *Brave New World* never went through the process at all, not that it would have mattered. The minister insisted that this book teaches promiscuity and drug use. My students who read the book see immediately that the novel is satirizing those things, but one cannot understand a book he hasn't read. I find it most ironic that a book that shouts so loudly against censorship has been restricted.

"I read a few pages and couldn't stomach any more," he said.

Parents flooded me with calls.

"How did *Brave New World* get on their list? I want my child to study this book," the parents said. "If we give permission, it'll be fine, right?"

"I don't know," I replied. "I'll go ask."

On November 5, I approached the board for clarification.

After a brief discussion, Mrs. Tillman told me, "Mrs. Ellis, if you have 100 percent written consent of the parents, you may teach whatever you want to, including these three books."

Back at school, my senior college preparatory students, many of whom were already 18—old enough to fight for this country, drive a car, and get into R-rated movies—prepared to read *Brave New World*. They brought me parental permission forms and enthusiasm.

Before we actually started reading the book, the ministers struck again, and on November 19, this same board took away the parents' rights to decide for their children. They summarily dismissed the fact that 100 percent of the parents had given consent for their students to read the book.

The school board said no.

When the discussions had first begun, the ministers adamantly insisted that parents be given more responsibility, more input. Now a mere five months later, the parents had been pushed aside. Now the two ministers who'd not read the books and had no children in school had been allowed by the board of education to usurp parental authority and direct English department curriculum.

"No books have been banned in this county," insisted board member Mrs. Joyce Tillman, when a reporter from Brunswick called her. "Students can still read them with parental permission."

No longer can Appling County college bound students study these three classics in the classroom. They are no longer available to our Honors English students or even to our most advanced students, the Advanced Placement British Literature class. Already, our rural students leave home for college at a disadvantage; their board of education saddled them with another enormous handicap.

Granted, the students can still check out the books, but without help, most of them cannot understand the multiple levels of meaning. These books require good teaching to help the students discover their underlying meanings. The students need my expertise, which the board forbade me to give. Paradoxically, I was hired for that very expertise.

Can I do my job without these books? I'll certainly do my best. I'll encourage them to read the banned books, and the very fact that people wanted them banned will engender curiosity. I, of course, will not teach them in class because the board, my official employer, has ordered me not to.

When I pick up any old Advanced Placement exam and look at the open-ended questions, I see a long list of books to choose from and more frequently than not, our forbidden three are there. My students and students across the whole country must take the AP Exam each year. I must prepare mine: I'd never send them off unprepared. However, they must take this exam without the same training afforded other students. Living in this small town here in the Bible Belt, my students have access to only two AP courses. When our students arrive at college, they will be sitting beside Atlanta students and others who've had eight or ten already, earning most of their core curriculum before ever graduating high school. Baxley students rarely have an opportunity even to see a play or attend a concert. We're a sports community, and support for the arts is sparse at best.

Therefore, I worry and fret, but I'm smart enough

to know that won't help my class at all. Instead, all my students jumped through the necessary hoops. Parents signed their forms or ordered *Brave New World* from Amazon.com. Throughout January, they read the novel, calling me at home if they needed help. On January 30, 2009, we met at the home of a student at his parents' invitation. Other parents attended too and were fascinated as the students conducted a Socratic seminar on this novel. They took it apart page by page, examining the deep meaning therein. Friday nights are my own to spend as I choose. That night I chose to teach.

It speaks volumes about their love of learning when Appling County's best students turn out on a Friday night to discuss a book. They sat in a circle on couches and on the carpet in deep discussion for nearly two hours before I stopped them for refreshments. In their enthusiasm, they had lost track of time as they talked about a society frighteningly comparable to ours. I wish Reverand Teutsch had joined us to see what this book is all about and how our best students handle it.

It also speaks volumes for the Appling County School Board when our students are forced to spend a Friday night studying one of the most highly acclaimed books of our age. *Brave New World* ranks fifth on a Modern Library list of the 100 best English-language novels of the 20th century.

As long as I keep teaching, I'll do whatever is necessary to encourage my students to read these books. I'll gladly give my time after school hours to assist them, but I've taught 32 years already and can retire any time. I plan to stay a few more years, but what then? Will Reverand Teutsch be on our doorsteps every time some child shows him a "dirty" word in a book? Will other teachers be so intimidated and fearful for their jobs that they will succumb to pressure? I couldn't blame them. School boards have been known to be vindictive and vicious if employees dare to disagree with them. The members of the Appling County School Board refused to back down and change their decision on these books even when their own lawyer told them they'd lose if someone sued, pointing out that the decision was based on religious beliefs.

Last month when Reverand Teutsch came with another book, *Grendel,* my stomach clenched again. Will it be Shakespeare next or Plath or Poe? I don't know, but I do know that I'll keep teaching as long as I can. Stress is a minor price to pay for such enthusiastic learning.

THE DREADED DYNAMIC:

A WHITE TEACHER'S STRUGGLES WITH RACE

Kelly Norris

M Y FIRST TEACHING job was at a high school in the crux of a sprawling six-way intersection in downtown Boston. Fruit trucks from a local company rumbled on and off a highway exit ramp next to the window, while inside the classroom sat kids who had immigrated from Afghanistan, Bosnia, Puerto Rico, Cambodia, Guatemala, and Tanzania. There were a few African American kids and a small number of white American kids as well.

In the throes of an identity crisis, I had returned from a year abroad in West Africa with braids and a disdain for anything too "white." What I didn't realize was how much my own whiteness, without close inspection, would inform my teaching and relationships with my students.

My first morning on the job, I sat in an oversized chair in the principal's office nervously passing my tumbler of coffee from hand to hand. It was midyear; the students, I was told, had "driven out" their teacher, who quit unexpectedly.

"Are you nervous?" My new principal asked me with brows furrowed. He was a petite man, burning with intensity.

"Yes."

"Good."

We took the elevator up to the third floor and he walked me across the hall to a classroom.

"You might find that these kids are—" he chopped the air with his hand. "No. Never mind. I want you to decide for yourself. They're your classes now." He did something like a small bow and stepped back into the elevator.

I was armed with a pile of photocopied chapters from *The House on Mango Street* by Sandra Cisneros, a plastic tub of magic markers, and three months of student-teaching experience under one of the best mentors I could hope for. The class was quiet but charged with energy as the bell rang and the students took their seats. I looked into faces I had not spent a lot of time looking into: all shades of brown and tan, some angular, some flat. There were smells, hairstyles, and fabrics that I didn't recognize. I introduce myself, passed out *Mango Street,* and plowed forward.

As I read through the text and gave writing prompts, they were quiet the whole period, trying hard to follow directions, holding everything in. Later in the semester, one of them admitted to me that they had all thought I was a discipline specialist brought in to restore order; we were mutually fearful.

After the first few days, our fear subsided and something else started to emerge. The bolder students tested me by talking out of turn and wandering over to friends in the middle of class. My *Mango Street* unit ran out. Standards and the state Massachusetts Comprehensive Assessment System test crept in.

At my first department meeting I was reminded that I needed to cover Elements of Fiction (page 18 in the textbook) and Literary Terms (page 26). When I brought out the textbook, I noticed that it pacified the students; they could remain quiet all period, answering the questions and copying elaborate dictionary definitions. This was tempting, though not what I had learned from my mentor, whose style was much more student-centered. She had used methods like the Socratic seminar to generate whole-class discussions on topics that interested the kids, and literature circles that had them working in small groups to discuss a text, each kid with his or her own, special role. She kept kids talking, not silenced. However, when I tried class discussions, everyone began talking out of turn and I couldn't control it, so I tried less and less. It wasn't something that the department emphasized anyway.

During preparatory time, I was teamed up with other teachers, all of us white, who shared the same students as me. We were meant to discuss the students' progress but the meetings quickly deteriorated into venting sessions where we dumped our frustrations on the kids:

"None of them want to learn."

"Why come to school if you're just going to sit there?"

"Do you know, not one of the Barahona's can read? The whole family is illiterate."

We shook our heads at the futility of it all.

The truth was I didn't know who my kids were. All I knew was that they weren't hitting the benchmarks I needed them to hit and because I thought I was doing a good job teaching, I began simply to dislike them for it. Like many of my colleagues, I figured if they couldn't learn from me then something must be wrong with them. As if to confirm my assumptions, the school discovered we had come out third from the bottom on a statewide list of MCAS scores. The MCAS test was used to determine the progress of not only students but schools as well. The short, stocky superintendent stood behind a podium at the next faculty meeting reciting numbers about annual yearly progress—a predetermined number of MCAS score points we needed to achieve—and all the funding we would lose if we didn't make it.

The school shifted into high gear and bore down into the crisis. We started holding extra MCAS prep classes anywhere we could—in the lunchroom, on the stage, in corners of the lobby sectioned off with partitions. Students were pulled from gym, art, and music. The curriculum was designed specifically to teach students how to answer questions in the format and style of the test: tricks and strategies for tackling multiple-choice questions and how to write an organized essay response with a five-sentence opening, three body paragraphs, and a closing.

With all of this formulaic teaching widening the distance I already kept from my students, it was almost impossible to see who they really were at all. For several weeks, I paced the aisles, barking instructions and going over all their wrong answers on practice MCAS tests. I thought I was being the kind of teacher I was supposed to be, but the permanent scowls on the kids' faces made me uneasy. How could I ever get back to the invigorating, joyful classrooms my mentor had modeled for me?

One Friday afternoon, while going over the latest MCAS practice, the kids began growing restless. I was restless, too. The class was boring; the work was empty. When we got to the bottom of a page, instead of turning to the next one I hesitated and glanced up at the kids. A moment went by while I just sat there, looking at them, bent over their desks. There was Ashley with her wavy, golden hair, olive skin, and perfectly applied pink lipstick. Lanky, pimple-faced Sean who wanted to go into the Marines. Reynaldo with the spiky hair already had his own business detailing cars. I took them all in.

Sensing the pause, they began to look up at me.

"What's wrong, Miss?" asked Ashley.

"Nothing," I smiled back at her, still gripping my packet. I could turn the page now, I thought. We could just keep moving ahead. Nevertheless, something in me resisted.

Sean capitalized instantly on the break from routine. "How old are you, Miss?"

"Twenty-three," I answered. "Why?"

He shrugged his shoulders. "My aunt's 24." He picked at the staple on the edge of his papers.

"I have a cousin who looks like you," said Ashley, putting her elbows on the desk and folding her hands together.

"Oh yeah?" I shifted in my seat, loosening my grip on the packet. "What's her name?"

We continued chatting and some of the shyer kids looked up suspiciously, wondering if we would get back to work.

"Our old teacher would never talk to us like this," Ashley announced.

Reynaldo seconded her with a grunt and a roll of his eyes.

"We were such a bad class, Miss," she continued, shaking her head. "The boys used to put tacks on his chair."

Reynaldo looked over his shoulder at his friend in the back row. "Remember when we set off those fireworks?"

My eyes widened. "Fireworks? What did you do that for?"

Reynaldo shook his head, letting out a thin stream of air like a leaky tire. "I don't know," he said finally, running his hand through his hair. Then as an afterthought: "He hated us."

It sufficed as an answer.

They had been through something, I realized, before I came. I hadn't even thought about that. When I heard they had "driven him out," I assumed they were bad kids, not that they had a very bad teacher.

Karla, a polite girl near the front, with long, dark hair and careful fingers, put her pencil down in the well at the top of her desk and smiled at me, recognizing my new presence. From the corner, Sopheap met my eyes. Sopheap's family had fled the genocide in Cambodia. He did not speak. The kids called him "No-peep." His vow of silence created a weight around him like the absence of a limb or a horrible scar across his face. Slight and self-contained, with a thin line of a mouth as if it had been drawn on, he glided around the classroom, head down, moving like air. His writing was so small and faint I could barely read it on the page. Was he made uneasy by this frank conversation? Sean got out of his seat to throw something away and lingered at the front of the room, which he quickly turned into a stage. "Hey, remember how he erased the board?"

There were nods and snickers as Sean picked up one of the erasers, held it to the board and marched to the other side with an extended arm, pushing the eraser across in a perfect straight line. He turned and went back, repeating the process just below the first line, his face drawn in mock seriousness. The class broke into laughter. I laughed, too, looking around, seeing the kids as if for the first time. One corner of Sopheap's mouth turned up in a half-smile, something I had never seen.

Next to me, Sean saw it, too. "Look!" he said, pointing with the eraser. "I made Sopheap laugh!" Sopheap ducked forward to hide his face, but we could see that both sides were now drawn in a smile and he was blushing tremendously. The bell rang and the students left class in a swirl of chatter.

"Have a good weekend, Miss," called Ashley, looking back over her shoulder.

The next year, the students began giving me things: Edwardo brought me back a miniature statue of a Goddess from Ecuador; Alicia wrote me a poem that I still have; Sam gave me forgiveness after a bad day when I kicked him out for frowning at me. I still had trouble with class discussion; however, my teaching softened until spontaneous conversations with my students were more frequent. We continued to do MCAS prep, but I began also to include units where the students chose their own books and I listened while they told me about them.

As I became closer to my students, the complexities of race and culture swirled in my head. Why were so many still failing? Could I ever really reach them as a white person? Awareness of the cultural divide between us undermined my convictions. I listened to hip-hop and had a group of friends that was diverse, but in my teaching, I still felt like part of the oppressive system; I was "the man." My mentor had been so great with our diverse group of kids—but she was also African American. Fears of enacting hidden prejudices paralyzed me, and I backed down easily, unable to take a stand in the classroom.

Midway through that second year, I was put into an MCAS prep class to assist another young, white English teacher with kids that were deemed "at risk" of failing the test. Standing at the front of the room with his cable-knit sweater and blond curls, Michael was the epitome of the prep school stereotype, blue eyes looking smugly through his glasses at the class. Some of my students from my regular English class were in the room. I noticed George right away from the pen cap that was sticking out of his mouth, a habit of his. He was one of the most vocal kids in my class, always the first to volunteer, and he glanced down, embarrassed, when our eyes met. The students were in absolute silence, dutifully copying down

Michael's own essay off the board. He wrote a sentence, thinking out loud as if he were alone in the room, and they waited for him to step aside so they could see it and write it down. Off to the side, I squirmed in my seat. These kids were capable of so much more, I thought. I hated Michael's assumption that they had nothing to work with, nothing to offer.

They were writing—or rather, he was writing, about a passage by Helen Keller in which she talks about revolution and a truly equal society. Unable to bear their silence, I stood up and posed a question to the class.

"What is she talking about here?" I asked.

The students just looked at me blankly. There was a wall of silence around them that had not yet been broken.

"Well, what do you think?"

No one dared answer. Michael stood with arms crossed at the back of the class, his mouth pursed in a tiny frown.

I called on the one student I knew would answer. "George?"

George coughed with surprise and took the pen cap from his mouth. He then answered tentatively, "Equality?"

At the end of class, as students filed out, Michael approached me. "I try not to engage them too much," he explained. "I give them very little wiggle room. I find that's all they can handle."

I took a deep breath in and asked if he thought copying his essays off the board was really going to help them.

"Oh, yes. One student came back last year and said she had memorized an entire essay of mine. Luckily, it was similar to the MCAS prompt that year and she was able to use it. She did very well."

Something about his self-assuredness, his materials spread comfortably around the room, the way he crossed his arms tightly over his chest while he spoke made me see the possibilities for myself. I didn't want to be that person.

I stayed exactly four years in that school, so I did get a chance to see some of my little freshmen grow into tall, young adults with deep voices and plans for the future. Sean signed up with the Marines. Ashley dyed her hair black and decided to pursue communications. Shamir, one of the few African American students I'd had, greeted me with a huge smile in the hallway just days before he was to graduate and I would be moving away from Boston. He and I had struggled during his sopho-more English class. He always wanted to go to sleep. I had tried waking him up and threatened to send him out of the room, but I was too afraid to confront him so I just gave up and left him there, head down all period. My fear was complex: I was afraid not only of him not liking me or of losing my authority if he refused, but of stepping into the uncomfortable role of white oppressor, or at least being seen that way. In an attempt to avoid that dreaded dynamic, I became more permissive than demanding. Somehow I thought this made me more "down" than other white teachers were. Shamir didn't pass the class, however, and my confidence in myself as an effective teacher was damaged.

It was spring outside and I could hear laughter and excited banter coming from the lunch room. "How are you, Shamir?" I asked.

"I'm good, Ms. Norris, how about you?"

"Fine. How's your English class?"

"Oh, it's okay. I have Mr. Kenny. I'm doing really good. I have an A, I think."

"Really? That's awesome. So I guess you're not sleeping in class…"

"No. Never."

That last answer hurt. What did Mr. Kenny have that I didn't?

"Then why'd you sleep in my class all the time?" I asked, jokingly, but part of me really wanted to know.

He grinned and looked me in the eye, answering with a little more wisdom than I'd expected. "Because you let me."

He headed down the stairs toward the cafeteria, dancing lightly over each step. "Bye, Miss," he called, without looking back.

WHATEVER IT TAKES

Lelac Almagor

I TEACH AT the Knowledge Is Power Program (KIPP).
Let me be the first to admit that these four words
are more essential to me than my hometown, my schooling, my writing, my discipline, or grade level. KIPP is
a nation of believers, of people who have dedicated
their daily lives to the conviction that they can teach
any child. That learning will make every child successful, and we have codified the catechism that gets our
students and us through that very long day: no shortcuts, no excuses. We are a team and family. If there is
a problem, we find a solution. At KIPP, if ever we are
failing—and the nature of our project is such that we
must come up short every day—we leap into action with
data, analysis, action steps, accountability; the vaunted

KIPP magic may be very simply that under such an eager onslaught almost any obstacle begins to fall to small and manageable pieces. Our signature line, our bravest banner, represents for me both our greatest strengths and our deepest uncertainties: *Whatever It Takes*.

For the most part, this is plainly true. I have known teachers, administrators, *and children* at my school to go to superhuman lengths to make school work. I know teachers who, in pairs, have gone to a student's home and waited outside until a guardian could be located to find out why a child wasn't making it in school. Then there was the time the principal picked kids up on her way to school after banging on their door for ten minutes until everybody was awake and organized. Our school day runs for nine hours from 7:45 AM to 5:00 PM. Tutoring, detention, and extracurricular activities run until 5:00 PM and are sometimes offered before school. There are also half-day enrichment classes on Saturdays, plus three weeks of summer programming. Teachers routinely continue working via school-issued phones and laptops long into the night. On any day, you can probably find at least a couple of teachers in as early as 6:30 AM and again, others lingering until 8:00 PM. We are also available to students on weekends and over vacations.

Many organizations make similar claims as KIPP, and do many of the same things we do, such as organizing their school day so that the kids spend long, uninterrupted periods actively reading, writing, and doing math—more so than memorizing facts, managing logistics, or negotiating behavior, all of which consumed large fractions of my own middle school experience—and caring intensely about the measurable gains that result. Media coverage of our school tends to seek out the iconic image of rows of African American children in brightly colored, tucked-in polo shirts demonstrating their learning in unison—it'd look militaristic if the kids weren't so darn happy—but, in fact, our instructional and disciplinary styles vary a great deal. Their uniting feature is unambiguous prioritization of student learning above all, most noticeably above convention or convenience, hence the *Whatever It Takes* motto. The hope is that we are also converging on a consensus about what works: not perfectly, not easily, not for every kid, not without fear of hubris, but our scores are high and our alumni are going to college.

We find moments in which to teach and learn during meals, in the hallways and bathrooms, and over the phone at night. Nevertheless, those of us who take these words most literally find ourselves wondering most often: What is *It*, exactly? How will we know *Whatever* when we see it? When is *Whatever* too much, or not enough?

In theory, *It* is easy: *It* is every KIPPster climbing the mountain to college—another motto, another bright banner—and middle-schoolers like Raynisha come to us needing only a little *Whatever* to get there. Raynisha is bubbly, bright, and absolutely hopeful. She and her mother, who is young but resolute, right away embraced the vision of honor roll, then boarding school, then college, and then the world. The outrageous injustice of her deficits in reading and math was made all the more apparent by the ease with which she caught up after only a few months of focused practice and feedback. There are still years of easy mastery separating her from the suburban kids with whom she'll be competing, but she's tough and confident, and she'll come to us for help if she needs it. Therefore, I don't worry much about Raynisha (though I know she is a miracle in her own right) as she toils her way to her well-earned spot in a before-and-after KIPP video. There are many like her.

However, there are also some like 13-year-old Mila. Mila, like Raynisha, is very bright. Like Raynisha, Mila comes to us with inexplicable unevenness in her academic skills; she is an avid and capable reader of young-adult literature who can't always decode one-syllable words like *poke* or *tank* out of context. Also like Raynisha, she talks well with adults and seeks out the company of her teachers outside of class. However, Mila hasn't accepted our sense of immediate urgency or our promises of future happiness. She rarely completes homework and spends most of the school day reading her book under her desk. Lately, she's developed the habit of wandering in and out of her classes, going to the bathroom without permission, or disappearing for 15 minutes between periods, stoically accepting disapproval, punishment, restriction, even suspension, and shrugging when she's asked if she even wants to attend our school. She lives with her father and stepmother, but they do not return phone calls or attend meetings unless we forbid Mila to return to school without them. Her teachers worry that she's depressed, and we line up what little counseling is available for her, but all we really have to offer to her is the rest of our program.

I know for certain that Mila is becoming a better reader—as much as she reads, how could she not? Nevertheless, I fear that reading alone isn't going to get her where she needs to go. We make plans and incentives and systems to get her to do her work, but we don't know how to make her see the purpose of it, and in some sense it might not be developmentally appropriate that we ask her to do so; when I was 12, it was my parents' job to value the long-term benefits of my education, and my job only to live up to their immediate expectations. We wonder if it'd be better for her, or saner for us, to let her fail—even to let her go—but we're not convinced she'd learn anything except failure from the experience. We don't know who will care for her after she leaves us, if we can't teach her to take care of herself. Even if *Whatever It Takes* isn't the right answer, it's the only answer we have. There are a handful of students like Mila, many of them boys.

There are also a handful like Taniqua. Taniqua can decode words rather fluently, but she has no idea what she's read, and she doesn't know she's missing anything;

she doesn't wonder where the meaning's gone when she can't find or remember it. When I sit and listen to her read aloud from a second grade-level text, she can talk her way through it, and we can build arguments from her flashes of insight if we rehearse each line aloud before we begin to write. I have seen children whose skills had been as severely stunted as this girl's—sometimes even for neurologically irreversible reasons—leave our school working at grade level by dint of pure daily grit over the course of four years of ten hours a day of something similar to intense physical therapy, only with a slower and less-tangible payoff. However, I have not yet found those hours for her or inspired her commitment to them. She has not yet qualified for special education services, and I have not yet lined up a tutor for her, for no good reason except—it hurts to type it, and to be typing when I ought to be *doing* it—that I have not gotten round to it. True *Whatever It Takes* would mean a lot more *Whatever* for this child.

A few weeks ago, we got three inches of ice and snow overnight, and school opened two hours late, and only about a dozen children showed up from each homeroom. We huddled together in the very front of the classroom, more casual and easy than we can usually afford, and I gave each pair of children long stretches of undivided attention. Watched them work out what they hadn't been able to when they'd been on their own, and at the end of the day I thought, what if *this* is *Whatever It Takes?*

What if I could guide every child perfectly if I had only 36 and not 85? What if I stayed up later, came in earlier, spent less time on other projects, and wasted fewer hours on nothing at all. Could I give a little more of this to all the children I teach? I know that is where the madness lies. Yet, I also know that I go home each day having done only 50 or 60 percent of what could have been done. There are parents I could have called, students I could have pulled aside for extra practice, quiet times when I checked my email instead of checking on a child, and lessons I left at good enough when 20 extra minutes might have made them unforgettable. Other teachers did more. Some children worked harder. Moreover, each of these omissions, individually, is easy to justify in the name of work-life balance, cost-benefit analysis, or long-term sustainability; but what if all of them, taken together, what if they are *Whatever It Takes?*

Finally, the darkest fear, for latest at night: What if my *Whatever It Takes* isn't what these children need at all? What if it is, in fact, as self-absorbed and self-aggrandizing a game as it sounds when I spell it out? What if it's more about the egos of competitive compulsives such as myself than about giving Taniqua, Mila, and even Raynisha the tools to make the most of their own lives? I can't promise without reservation that the kind of smartness we offer will get them through college, nor can I guarantee that college will bestow upon them dignity or peace. If I ever work that 100 percent magic, if I get every one of my students demonstrably reading at what we've decided to call the seventh-grade level, how many of those students will have been brought closer to the fierce joy I will surely experience on that day?

I get up again in the morning, though, on the strength of a couple of leaps of faith that don't quite fit on T-shirts. First: I do believe, in the bright light of day, that what makes life difficult for my children's families is largely a lack of professional and personal skills, and that the desire to give those skills to their children is what motivates them to stay at our school despite the often-inconvenient intensity we bring into their lives. Though this desire is neither constant nor uncomplicated, it is shared among all of us, and it transcends whatever selfishness any of us bring to it.

Second: I know absolutely that every child can acquire these skills—I have learned from watching miracles—and I believe that only time and persistence are required to unlock them in each one. If I haven't found the way yet, I still can, any morning between now and the end of June.

Third: I accept that what is in our power to grant is not enough for every child, cannot be fully granted to every child we serve, and that we serve both too many children and not enough. Nevertheless, I believe that we are giving almost all of our students something that is good, necessary if not sufficient, and I am willing to hope that no such gift will go entirely unused.

Fourth: I own that I am not doing as *much* as I could. If I did more, I might not last as long. However, what I do, I do in the best way that I know how (also a KIPPism) with the utmost creativity, patience, and thoughtfulness that I can muster, and I try to learn and improve, so that my 50 or 60 percent means a little more each year.

And finally: When I can't fall asleep, or I can't leave the building at night, I get up and go do one more thing—one phone call, one individualized assignment, five minutes of listening to a quiet child speak—that I know is good and that I hope like hell is this day's *Whatever*. I have learned to let that be enough.

‖

LOFTY IDEALS

Ebony Elizabeth Thomas

A NEW TEACHER'S induction into the field involves
many trials by fire. One must learn how to deliver
curricular content effectively, build a classroom community of learners, and manage many interpersonal relationships with parents, administrators, and peers. However,
in my experience, the flames that burn the hottest usually involve grading. All of the management challenges
that I have faced since I began teaching a decade ago
have been traceable to a grading dispute—all of them.

Of course, as a pre-service teacher at Florida Agri-
culture and Mechanical University (FAMU), I was
confident that I knew exactly when and how to assess
student learning. FAMU is one of the largest producers
of African American teachers in the nation. Its teacher

preparation program is very traditional and very thorough. Not only had I taken a class entitled Measurement and Evaluation," each of my other courses in education required authentic assessments for every unit plan that I completed. For example, for my Introduction to Educational Technology course, we had to design a multimedia assessment for our future students. During the 1998–1999 school year, my group conceived an interactive teacher newsletter for students and their parents that was seen as quite cutting edge. In Adolescent Literature and English Methods, we created unit plans and designed traditional multiple-choice assessments with essay options. In Secondary School Literacy, we learned how to give entering students reading and writing assessments and use portfolios in middle school and high school classrooms. Between these and other courses, as well as practicum and student teaching experiences, I had an excellent academic foundation for classroom teaching.

As I theorized about the kind of teacher I would eventually become, I decided that above all else I wanted to be fair. One of my pet peeves as a student had been observing high school peers who were able to sweet-talk teachers into giving them an A– instead of a B+. After doing this, they ended up with higher grade point averages than those of us who worked hard and took our knocks when report cards were mailed home. Even in postsecondary classes, there were always some folks who wanted to bend the rules. It wasn't that they couldn't do the work. For them, education wasn't a matter of learning, shaping their intellectual and ethical character. It was a depersonalized transaction. *Tell me what I need to do to get an A,* they said. That was why I would never bend the rules for my students, I told myself. Otherwise, I would be contributing to the degeneration of society.

I kept my lofty ideals until I administered the first math quiz in my fifth grade language arts and mathematics homeroom in September. I had snagged a great teaching position working with motivated children and preteens in one of the nation's poorest urban districts. I spent several weeks toward the end of the summer preparing my classroom for my students, and soon was off to a great start. Very pleased with my efficient grading system in particular, I showed it to one of my mentors upon his request. My traditional, dark green grade book and lesson plan book by Ward were neat and color-coded with specific highlighters and ink. My management binder featured an informational page for every student with a dossier on the front and a log for notes and dates of phone calls on the back. I was proud of the fact that I had called nearly 100 students' homes during the first two weeks of classes, just as I had been taught by my education school professors. I introduced myself to the parents, explained the accelerated talented and gifted (TAG) curriculum, and answered their questions.

Yet my mentor wasn't very interested in the fancy trappings of my organizational ability. He was most interested in the grades I was giving the kids. He shook his head and told me: "No, this just isn't going to work. More than half of these kids failed the test. You have to let them take the test over." I protested that it wasn't fair, that the students had plenty of time to practice, and most of the failing grades were earned by kids who hadn't completed their class and homework problems. Of course, students who chose not to practice math skills would not do well on tests. At the time, I was not thinking about *why* the students hadn't completed their homework, worked at different paces, or only worked well when I was sitting next to them in class. Like many new teachers, I was teaching them as I had been taught, and because it worked for me, of course, I believed it would work for my students.

"You have to retest," my mentor urged me. "Parents at this school aren't going to let you fail their kids." When I asked what should be done if the students failed a second time, he told me, "You either keep testing them until they get it, or you grade on a curve." I was appalled, but decided to trust him. However, a little bit of my idealism faded away on that day.

No sooner had I loosened my standards a bit to accommodate the political climate than I ran into my first student who wanted to game the system: Queen McCall. Queen was the daughter of a district administrator. This was her first year in the accelerated program. Ever since the beginning of the school year, I had been monitoring

Queen's progress in my language arts and math classes. Like many of my new students, she was struggling academically. Her other core subject teachers came to me often expressing their concerns about her performance in science, social studies, and elective classes. Mrs. McCall, her mother, shared with me that Queen had some health problems, so I let her go to the lavatory and the office whenever she needed to in my class. I was confident that I had developed a successful relationship with Queen and her parents—or so I thought.

Early one morning, Queen told me that she lost her backpack. Concerned, I contacted the main office. The staff promptly made a PA announcement about it. Later that week, I asked Queen whether or not her bag was found. She said that it was on a neighbor's porch. I told her that I was glad and chalked it up as a problem solved.

The very next day after the book bag was reported missing, I returned a multiplication test to every member of the class who was present. The highest grade in the class was a C. Rather than throw out the test completely, I told the students to go home, correct their answers, and bring them back the next day for a homework grade. Queen was there, and received her test. The class received explicit and detailed instructions about what was to be done. "Now that we've worked through similar problems, you guys seem to be on the right track!" I said. "Now it's your turn. For homework, please redo any problem that is marked with an 'X' or 'half-credit.' If you do that, you will get a higher grade on your test!" Twenty-five students completed their test corrections by the next day, and all but Queen and one other student complied in time for Friday's weekly progress reports.

It was my classroom policy to make personal contact with students when collecting any assignment. When I asked Queen what happened to her math test, she said, "It was in my book bag."

I asked her, "Didn't you find your book bag the other day?" She told me no. Then I told her that what she was saying couldn't be true because the test was returned *after* the book bag was missing. She shrugged and looked away. That afternoon, I made sure to note the missing test and book bag on her progress report. I also expressed my concerns about Queen's grades in all of her core subjects.

The next week, Queen returned her weekly progress report. Mrs. McCall wrote on the back of the report that she didn't have any idea that Queen's grades were so low, and to please allow her to make up the math test. A couple of days later, Mrs. McCall came to talk with me before school. She stated that Queen believed that her locker partner, Kiana Mitchell, had been taking Queen's books home, erasing Queen's name in the books, and putting her own in its place. I was unsure of how to deal with the incident, because Kiana was not at school yet (she was absent that day). I assured

Mrs. McCall that I would be sure to speak with both girls when Kiana arrived.

The next morning, Mrs. McCall's demeanor was not nearly as accommodating. She stormed into my classroom and stood behind my desk. "May I speak with you for a minute, Ms. Thomas?" she asked.

"Sure, but it'll have to be a quick minute," I replied. "It's almost 8:30, and I have to let the students in and take attendance."

I stepped outside of the classroom. Mrs. McCall then began to explain that she encouraged her children to ask questions while in class. She said that Queen told her that she told me "I don't understand" and I told her "you don't understand anything." That statement is so completely contrary to who I am as a person and a teacher that I immediately denied it. My frustration with this situation turned into anger. I told Mrs. McCall, "I know Queen is your daughter, but she has not told the truth before." I then quickly related the incident of the math test.

Mrs. McCall became a little upset. "Oh, yeah? What date was the book bag lost, then?" she asked me.

"I don't know, ma'am!" I replied. "I have over 100 students! I'll have to check my records." I excused myself because nothing profitable would have come out of the situation, and I had to get back to work.

"I don't appreciate that you're telling my daughter she's stupid, and now you're telling me she's a liar. I think we need to have a parent conference," Mrs. McCall said. I agreed, and suggested that Queen's other teachers and an administrator participate. She said, "No, this first time I think you and me and my husband need to have a conference alone."

That was the beginning of a long and contentious relationship with the McCalls. Queen spent the rest of the school year avoiding assignments, and then telling her parents the most outrageous lies about her classmates and me. The worst of all was when I ruined a student-teacher mentorship with one of my best students when I asked her to collaborate with Queen. I thought that Courtney's work ethic and good citizenship skills would rub off on Queen. To the contrary, within a week Queen had the girl in tears after a note-passing slander campaign. Of course, Courtney's mother called the school and demanded a conference, and then rightfully questioned my judgment in exposing her daughter to such a manipulative little girl. Courtney never forgave me. Neither did her mother.

Perhaps I could have avoided these disasters with a bit more maturity. However, there was nothing in my certification program that could have prepared me for my first year's experience with Queen and the McCalls. My vice principal later told me that he believed Queen was a pathological liar; I chose to shrug and chalk up the unpleasantness with the McCalls to my status as a novice. New teachers believe that they are going into the classroom to teach kids like those in the textbooks and on television, not necessarily little people who have interests and needs that they are attempting to meet.

Since Queen, I have faced occasional grading challenges. Two years later, as a new high school English teacher, there was an 11th grade Advanced Placement student who protested to the department chair against my strict scoring policies and heavy workload. ("She's not fair!" "She doesn't return papers fast enough!") There was the senior news magazine student whose mother called the district superintendent because the student rarely attended class or completed articles, her supervising student editors recommended a lower grade, and I gave it to her. ("How can she let children grade other children?" "She doesn't know what she's doing!") In creative writing, there was plagiarism almost every semester. ("It was just too hard!" "She just doesn't understand!")

My grading dilemmas became less frequent only when I accepted a veteran colleague's advice to "be myself." Since I was barely of legal age when I began to teach, it took most of the next few years to figure out exactly what "being myself" meant. In order to be myself as a teacher, I had to figure out what I valued and what I thought education was all about. By my fourth year in the classroom, I knew that being myself meant foregrounding a social justice perspective in my teaching. This perspective positioned students as experts on their own experiences, collaborators in the classroom, and co-creators of school and community culture. With my students, I experienced and wrote about September 11, marched against the war in Iraq before it began, and protested against Proposal E. Several innovative students and I began a school newsmagazine, and after an investigative reporter from the local ABC affiliate showed up in my classroom hallway one morning, I used my knowledge of journalism from my days as a campus columnist at FAMU to help students learn how to construct exposés. We read young adult literature, went to the library to learn more about the contemporary social issues that the genre touches upon, and wrote papers that were relevant to students' lived experiences. We even went overseas together because I insisted to them that it was impossible to understand what it was like to be African American, Palestinian, Bangladeshi, Mexican, Hmong, or Caucasian in America if you could not analyze America from a distance as a social construct, and not as normative.

By the time I reached the end of my induction period, I felt strongly that teaching should empower students and provide them with real agency, so that they would not feel trapped by the circumstances of their birth, but transcend all expectations. This radically changed my perspective on what students should know and do on conventional assessments.

By the time I left my first district, the majority of my

students saw my classes as vibrant and relevant to the way they experienced the world. In particular, they found it very empowering that I always negotiated authority with them. "You are young adults," I'd tell them. "You should know how to run this classroom if I am not here." (Inevitably, by mid-October, they were able to do this. Once, when I was out sick and there was a glitch in the SubFinder system, it was early afternoon before anyone realized I was out.) Even the curriculum was up for negotiation in quarterly town hall meetings, a teaching strategy that I used successfully with fifth through twelfth graders. "Here's what the state and the district say you have to learn," I'd say. "In addition, there's much that I feel is important for you to learn. Now, what would you *like* to learn?" I listened to them, and would adjust accordingly. Students felt as if I took their points of view seriously, and appreciated the fact that I readily shared authority. In turn, they positioned me as an expert on what they needed to know in order to succeed in the wider world, and accepted my mentorship and care as genuine. Some teachers were their "other mothers"; due to my youth and proximity to their ages, I became their "big sister." It has been an honor and a privilege to keep in touch with many of them, and to see what wonderful young adults they have become.

My grading challenges have become the exception and not the rule. I have found that being fair, firm, and consistent works with the vast majority of students.

Moreover, when kids and teens respect you, believe that you know what you are doing, and trust that you have their best interests at heart, there are always many opportunities to exercise grace. Knowing when and how best to exercise grace is one small part of the career-long task of learning to teach.

THE JOYS AND
SORROWS OF TEACHING
HIGH SCHOOL ESL:
SARANGEREL'S STORY

Susan R. Adams

ENGLISH AS A second language (ESL) teachers lead fascinating lives. We have the privilege of working closely with students from many countries, richly diverse cultures, and a cornucopia of languages and dialects. Our students and their families move to pulses and beats that are not always discernable to us until we get to know them and their families, learn their stories, and understand their dreams and desires. Until we do the hard work of listening, asking good questions, not making assumptions, and digging into these stories, most of us know we are not really reaching and teaching the whole child; and of course, this entire process is complicated enormously by the number of languages spoken by our students.

Contrary to popular misconception, ESL teachers do not speak all of the languages of their students. Mainstream teachers often bring non-English speaking students to me, sigh, and say, "Could you talk to her? She does not understand a word I am saying!" I then proceed to explain in simple English what the teacher had been trying to say, and the mainstream teacher is almost disgusted when it works. "Well! *I* could have done that!" is a common response. "Why *didn't* you if it is so easy?" is what I always want to say. Many of us speak some of the more common languages, especially Spanish, but few of us are prepared to speak the languages of those groups with small representation. I speak Spanish and can manage fairly well with other Romance languages, but I am no match for African or Asian languages with which I have no experience as a learner. I often have students from four continents, speaking 12 different languages. The vast majority of my students are Spanish-speakers, and we communicate pretty well. Others have been from French-speaking African nations and we found a way to get our points across. Sometimes a student has arrived speaking a language that is new and seems obscure in our community. Take, for example, Mongolian.

Sarangerel, who was promptly renamed Sara by the other teachers in my urban Indianapolis high school, came to our school in late February. She had only been in the United States for about six months, but had already attended at least three other schools that we could verify. She was 17 years old, extremely courteous, slender, dark-eyed with a spark of determination and humor, reserved with the other students, and highly motivated to do well in our school.

Sarangerel worked hard to adapt to the ways of our urban, mostly African American high school quickly, and it was clear to all of her teachers that she had already taken many of the traditional high school courses in her native Mongolia, but that she struggled to communicate her deep knowledge in English. While she floundered in U.S. history due to a lack of background knowledge and a textbook written in college-level English, she excelled in math and science, especially when she could demonstrate her skills in numbers or diagrams.

She was a joy in class, always checking to make sure that she was doing what the teachers wanted, somehow always exceeding expectations in spite of her beginner's status in English. At the end of every class period, she would approach the teacher with anxious eyes, insistent that we tell her how she had done and what she could do better next time. This practice set her apart for two reasons: Most students made a mad dash for the door at the bell to soak up some social time in the hall and it made her late to almost every class, but she had a way of smiling shyly and smoothing her tardiness over with teachers. Somehow we just could not penalize her for caring so much about her own learning.

Because Sarangerel had already been enrolled in three other U.S. schools, she had learned some English, so while our conversations were slow and stilted, we were mostly able to understand each other in simple terms. I was able to schedule two class periods of ESL a day with her, with our long-term plan being to have her graduate high school at the end of the following year. Sarangerel was very clear in her mind that she was headed to college and we all believed her. She worked tirelessly on every task I laid before her, preferring to work alone and to write instead of working collaboratively with the other ESL students in the room. Sarangerel worried constantly that she was not making enough progress and that her spoken English was not pleasing me.

Although her mother had accompanied her to our school when Sarangerel was enrolled, it was impossible to communicate directly with her mother, who spoke no English. No one in our district was readily available to translate, so we muddled through, assisted by Sarangerel's previous enrollment experiences in other schools and by her sincere effort to understand what we said. When I sat down with her to complete the enrollment forms and to go over her transcripts, I attempted to understand why she had already been in so many schools in so few months. We did everything we could to communicate such complex explanations to each other; anyone watching us would have thought we were playing Charades, or even Win, Lose or Draw. Sarangerel endured this tedious process with a gentle smile, great patience, and a keen sense of humor as I ruled out migrant worker status and other employment explanations for the frequent moves. Every question I asked seemed to come back to "friends live there" and after a while I let it go.

Less than one month after Sarangerel arrived, our annual state assessment rolled around. In spite of the fact she had been enrolled less than one year, she insisted on taking it. I was convinced that she had a chance at passing the math portion of the test if she could decode enough of the text in order to solve the problems. I had given this test many times and I had seen ESL students who knew far less math than Sarangerel pass the test, which is basically a ninth grade algebra and beginning geometry test. The test is composed of two parts: a multiple-choice, number-crunching component, and a far more difficult, extended-response component. Sarangerel labored intensively over the test, sailing easily through the multiple-choice portion and then bogging down over the extended response questions, which required her to decode the story problem, show her work, and often, and explain her answers.

Long after the other students had finished the test and left, Sarangerel plugged away determinedly, sometimes crying quietly when she ran into scenarios she could make no sense of. Although the test designers claim our assessment has been rigorously examined for cultural biases, that year's test was a running series of story problems based on a high school preparing for homecoming, a distinctly middle-class American tradition, and one not always practiced in urban high schools. We had celebrated homecoming in early October at my school, but most of my students had largely ignored it, seeing no reason to participate in such activities as screaming pep sessions in the gym or sitting in the cold to watch American football. If we had only known that homecoming was going to be on the test, I would have insisted they pay attention!

My other students had balked over the same homecoming scenario and many had quietly pleaded for me to explain what the storyline was talking about, which I am not permitted to do during state assessment testing. Testing is always a painful experience for the students and the ESL teachers alike. I knew that all I had to do was explain in rough terms what homecoming is, and then most of them could have easily answered the story problems. I knew from working closely with their math teachers that they had mastered the math skills necessary to pass this part of the test. What they could not do was make sense of the scenarios and communicate their responses in the kind of English required by the test.

On the test, there were questions about the amount of lumber needed for building parade floats, how much space would be set aside for crowds, and other details lost on this young Mongolian woman who had never even witnessed homecoming. I knew without a doubt that Sarangerel could do far more than the test required if it were in Mongolian, but I paced the classroom and chewed my fingers anxiously, hoping she could sift through the unnecessary details and solve the simple math problem underneath. Finally, she sighed, closed the book, wiped her eyes, and smiled at me. I hugged her, sent her home, and hoped her brilliance would be apparent to the graders.

About two weeks later, Sarangerel's mother appeared in the doorway of my classroom. This did not surprise me; parents of English language learners (ELLs) often bypass the main office and go straight to the ESL classroom in hopes that they will be welcomed and understood there. Going into the office meant that our well-intended secretary would shout "Wait here! I will get Ms. Adams!" repeatedly as she picked up the phone to call me, leaving them to wait helplessly in the corner. As Sarangerel glanced up and saw her mother in the door, her face fell. As we both walked to the door, I muttered, "What is going on?" She said, "We moving tomorrow." My other students got quiet and pretended to do their work, but were listening intently so that later they could pass on the *chisme* (Spanish for gossip) correctly and with juicy details to their friends. They were accustomed to parents wanting to speak with me, but those visits were generally to deal with behavior problems, and Sarangerel was never in trouble, so they were very curious.

I invited her mother inside our classroom door, where I could keep my eye on my students but maintain a respectable distance away from them. Her mother was dressed like a professional business woman in a suit jacket, skirt, nylons, and heels, although they were a few years out of fashion and might have been bought at Goodwill instead of Macy's. I felt frumpy indeed in my ubiquitous denim jumper, orthopedic shoes, and with my decidedly inelegant school ID around my neck. With Sarangerel's translation help, I told her mother how well Sarangerel had adapted to our school, how all her teachers adored her, how hard she worked, and how happy everyone was to have Sarangerel in our school. My students stayed calm, quietly listening to this exchange, which was all usual fare for parent conversations in my classroom. Her mother beamed as Sarangerel gave her the short and modest Mongolian version of my praise.

I put on my best, authoritative, take-no-prisoners teacher face and cut to the chase, insisting firmly that her mother reconsider moving, pointing out that we only had six weeks of school left and that Sarangerel's grades would suffer in the move. Her mother smiled politely and insisted that they were indeed moving tomorrow to be closer to friends in Virginia. Clutching at straws, I blurted, "What about your friends here? Couldn't Sarangerel stay with them until the end of the semester?"

At this her mother hesitated, but then replied that all their local friends were males and it would be inappropriate for Sarangerel to remain with them. Frantically racking my mind for solutions, I resorted to begging, "Please, *please* do not move Sarangerel again! You have no idea how difficult it is for her to keep changing schools, and she is too respectful to tell you. You are being very selfish! She is doing well here, and she needs to finish the year with us! You need to stay here for Sarangerel just a few more weeks!"

At this emotional outburst, Sarangerel stopped interpreting, too uncomfortable to tell her mother what I had said, and physically moved away from her mother and me. Then the craziest thing happened. With no one translating, Sarangerel's mother began explaining in Mongolian how difficult their transition to the United States had been for the parents, how they had looked high and low for work that would support the family, how desperately lonely they were for their home, family, and friends in Mongolia, and how worried they were about providing a good future for Sarangerel.

By now we were both weeping openly, clutching each other while Sarangerel and her classmates watched with gaping mouths. No translation was necessary. This was one of those moments where things just work, where our essential humanness is our real connection, and where stopping to translate would have meant a loss of nuance, intention, and depth of feeling. Our fears and frustrations gushed out, and we somehow understood each other deeply and completely. Finally, after we had each poured out our hearts in our own languages, with me taking one more chance to try to explain how difficult it is on kids to be jerked in and out of schools, we smiled, wiped our eyes, laughed a little, and hugged each other fiercely.

I turned to Sarangerel, apologized for embarrassing her, and told her how deeply sorry we all were to lose her, that we loved her and wanted the best for her. After many good-byes and a few more tears, Sarangerel and her mother went to the office to officially withdraw her from our school and arrange for a transfer to the fifth school number in Sarangerel's short U.S. journey. Shaken, I returned to my students who were so quietly stunned by the drama they had just witnessed that they said nothing, most of them avoiding eye contact with me. We were all saddened by the loss of our new friend, Sarangerel, and we all sensed the fragility of our being together, knowing we could lose someone else tomorrow.

Three weeks later, I received notification that Sarangerel had passed our state math assessment. I wished I could have celebrated this victory with her and could have savored the triumph of overcoming a test designed to trip her up, but I sat quietly picturing her in her new school, and hoping those new teachers were loving her and realizing her potential. For me, this is the epitome of what it means to be an ESL teacher; we suffer so many painful losses and few bittersweet wins. We laugh and cry with people who do not speak our language or understand our school systems, but who long for something better with us. We taste the magic of transcending borders and reaching out to one another across differences. There is no other teaching job quite like this.

THE PRESSURES OF TEACHING

Sandra Cohen

WHEN I BECAME a high school math teacher six years ago, I had to learn to multitask in a completely new way. In the past, multitasking was doing my nails while watching a television show. Now, in 45 minutes, I had to teach a lesson, take attendance, keep all of the students on-task, be entertaining, and be prepared for interruptions such as being handed a slip of paper requiring me to "cover" for a colleague who fell ill in the middle of class. Of course, this does not include the inevitable announcements over the speaker system, the fire drill, a student in the hallway begging to talk to his/ her friend for just a minute, a student wanting to search the room for a lost personal item, and the favorite: when the principal shows up unannounced with a group of half a dozen visitors and says, "Just pretend we're not here."

The only thing that my education classes prepared me for was keeping the students on task. We were taught that if the lesson was interesting, then the students would respond. This is somewhat true, but there are some students who will never be engaged even if I teach while standing on my head. I find that what keeps them on task is when they have something to gain by paying attention, such as knowing there will be a quiz at the end of the period or a test the next day. Even the promise of getting a stamp or a sticker at the end of the lesson works (even in high school). However, nothing engages them more than knowing about a teacher's personal life. So, when I relate slope to my having a fight with my husband because he took me hiking up an extremely steep hill, believe me, they're all interested.

Now, thinking back to when I began teaching, I realize that I went through a process that I had to go through. There are no shortcuts to learning how to become a teacher. During my first year, I learned a lot about what to do and what not to do. Things to do include: get to work very early so you can be organized before classes start, make lesson plans at least one week in advance, try all problems before assigning them to the class, time yourself and pretend you're taking a test you will be giving, observe other teachers, talk to other teachers, and stay out of trouble. Inevitably, there is always a clique of teachers that the administration is not fond of. Do not hang out with them until the administration knows you well enough to know that you can think for yourself. I sought advice from a broad spectrum of teachers who gave me extensive resources to fall back on. Because I started teaching later in life, I was a bit more comfortable in my own skin and a little freer opening up to others and asking even the stupidest question.

Sometimes I wondered why the students put up with me. Didn't they realize that I had no idea what I was doing? Although mathematics has always come easily to me, teaching it is a whole other thing. Students will come up with questions that I never thought about, and it's hard not to look like an idiot when 30 students are waiting for an answer that you don't have. My colleagues advised me that when I didn't know an answer to a question that I should offer it an extra credit project for that night, and it would get me off the hook for the moment. Years later, gaining confidence as a teacher, I took no issue admitting that I didn't know the answer and would transform the moment into a teaching opportunity. Together, we would access the Internet on the Smart Board and research the problem. Nevertheless, when I first began teaching, it was possible that my students felt sorry for me and gave me a break. It's akin to making fun of a sibling but having no tolerance for anyone else making fun of him or her. When students see things aren't going well, they are sometimes mature beyond their years and will reach out to help.

What I was not prepared for as a novice—and what still sometimes surprises me—was the different personalities I would have to deal with. High school students can be surprisingly mature yet very sensitive at the same time. Many are looking for a role model because they don't have one at home. Many will confide their most personal secrets, which puts a greater responsibility on me to be consistent. They may have no consistency in their home lives and crave knowing that things will be the same no matter what. Some teenagers are physically and sexually abused and will often place a huge amount of trust in you. If they disclose something that I must disclose, and I explain to them that I have to report the situation to a third party, they seem relieved.

They know I follow the rules and that's probably why they came to me in the first place. I had a situation in which a student was clearly being abused at home and although I reported it to other staff, I was instructed by my union representative to report it to child services as well, which I did. Whether it was pure coincidence or not, the next day, the parent called me to see how her child was doing. While I wanted to scream at her and tell her that I knew what she had done, I had to remain professional and act as if I didn't know anything.

The bottom line is that all high school teenagers want

consistency, discipline, and to be treated fairly. So many times I thought that I had been too harsh in my reaction to a situation, but the next day, the student greeted me in the hallway as if nothing had happened. It's like when a parent yells at a child; the child is mad at them for the moment, but the fact is that this is his or her parent and staying mad is not an option.

Being a parent has helped me be a better teacher. Sometimes, all it takes is a look my students call "the mother look." It's that look of disappointment that embarrasses them and usually stops the bad behavior. I have learned from parenting my own children that if I give in, I'm done. Therefore, I stick to my guns whether it is refusing to teach or assigning a huge project. Usually, this is something that I will only have to do once to get my message across, but just as it is difficult to do as a parent, it is just as difficult to do as a teacher.

Students may say that they dislike a class because the teacher has no control over it. I will hear a student in my class say to another student, "At least I can learn something in this class. In Mr. So-and-so's class, we can't learn anything because the kids are so bad and don't listen to him." While I would have thought students would like that because it gives them free reign in the classroom, the exact opposite is true. They might not show it, but they want to learn. There's nothing better than hearing a student say, "I feel so smart," as he or she leaves the class. In fact, I tell each of my incoming

Advanced Placement calculus classes something a former calculus student said: "When I'm doing calculus, I feel like the stupidest person in the world, but when I can solve a problem, I feel like the smartest person in the world." Moreover, if you challenge the students and keep them engaged, they will respond.

I have had many students who seemed to torture me every day in the classroom. They'd walk into class late, loud, wanting everyone to look at them (which of course they do). Others will start complaining that I don't call on them enough. There is a never-ending list of reasons students have to complain, and while I know they hate me at the time, they will come to me the following year or when they graduate to tell me that I was the only one who held them up to a standard that no one else thought they could reach. In fact, I had one student for two years in a row who hated me. I know this because he told me all of the time. If he was talking during class and I asked him to stop, he would ask, "Why do you hate me?" If I spoke to him about his bad behavior, he would say, "You know I hate you and you hate me. Why can't you just leave me alone?" He is now a senior and recently came to me to tell me that he was just awarded a full scholarship for college based on an essay he wrote about me. Apparently, he wrote about how he never thought he would succeed and how, while he hated me at the time, he can now reflect back and realize that I taught him not to settle for less and to question why if I believed in him, he didn't believe in himself. I was shocked when he told me this, and all of the misery he'd caused me seemed to melt away. It's like childbirth: you say you'll never go through it again, and then as time passes, you realize it may have been worth it.

It is memories like that that make me return as a teacher each year. Teaching can sometimes be so overwhelming, but I have found that the secret is in taking it one day at a time and not taking things personally. A teacher from my department hit it right on the head when he recently had a bad day. He said, "We're like monkeys in a zoo. You stand in front of a class and students say terrible, mean things to you, and you just have to wipe it off your face and come back the next day and act like it never happened." He's so right. Sometimes I feel like I should win an Academy Award for the composure I maintain. It's easy to focus on the bad aspects of teaching rather than the good but, at the end of the day, I can always smile about something funny or heartwarming that happened in class, and I guess that's what keeps me coming back every year.

"F's" Instead of "Not Yets"

Win Radigan

JASON WALKED INTO my writers' workshop class three days into the new cycle. I initialed his program card, handed him the grading policy and course outline, and watched him saunter to the back of the room where he slouched into a seat in the farthest corner. No notebook, no pencil, no paper—just Jason—a tall gangly teen chewing on a toothpick and wearing a hooded jacket. In the days that followed, Jason did little work even when supplied with pen and paper. This was his second attempt at the required ninth grade class. His success did not look promising.

One day, however, when I was teaching how to

narrow a topic into a thesis statement for outlining, researching, and writing a essay with correct footnotes and a bibliographic citation, I called on Jason.

"What's your topic?" I asked.

Jason stopped chewing long enough to say, "Sex," with a challenging air.

"What about it?" I shot back. "Are you interested in homosexual or heterosexual sex? Normal or abnormal practices? Teen sex, premarital sex, safe sex?"

Jason sputtered around the ubiquitous toothpick, "Normal!"

"Okay," I replied. "Try thinking of a question you want to answer. I will be around in a couple of minutes."

I checked in on students as they grappled with formulating a research question and a thesis statement to prove or disprove. My private couple of minutes with Jason seemed to spark some curiosity. In the classes that followed, we visited the library to do research with the librarian's help. Students outlined their essays, which they handed in for feedback. I collected homework in the form of note cards and correct citation, taught how to avoid plagiarism, and collected, corrected, and graded every step of the way. Jason handed in the class work, but not any homework.

At the end of the course, he stopped into the English office where I was just bubbling in class grades and comments and asked, "So, Teach, did I pass?"

"I'm sorry, Jason. There was just not quite enough work."

"That's all right," he said. "I didn't think so, anyway."

I felt sad and helpless as he walked away with his friends. I had failed him, and I did not know then what I could have done differently given the pressures and constraints of the system.

That was more than 25 years ago and, sadly, from my current work with teachers and supervisors, I could be talking about today. In 1982, I felt constrained by a grading system and an artificial time frame that seemed the norm. I had 170 students in five classes—three sections of writers' workshop and two of short story. I had a building assignment working in the college office one period a day. I was lucky in that the school had a flexible schedule that built in a little extra time on some days by having classes meet in four-day weekly "bands" of two one-hour classes and two 40-minute periods. Therefore, occasionally I had two hours free during the day for lunch and preparation instead of the conventional 80 minutes.

Like most of my colleague English teachers, I had to spend most evenings and weekends grading papers or planning lessons. Planning meant not only reading and re-reading the stories I was teaching, but also reading the literary criticism and author biographies, and developing tasks for students that would hook them into reading the stories for character, plot, theme, conflict, style, point of view, and so on. I tried to develop questions and activities that would help students make connections to their lives or current television or film, prepare vocabulary lists, sequence lessons in writing, and use student work to guide the teaching of rhetorical conventions. I also spent a good chunk of the summer outlining the upcoming term's courses—if I was lucky enough to know my program in advance.

Grading as many as 400 papers per week, I often resorted to a system of √, √-, or √+ with comments such as "Good job," "More detail," or "See me." Sometimes, I resorted to multiple-choice quizzes to make grading easier, rather than the pieces of writing that more effectively captured what students knew and could do. At times, papers piled up and I scurried at the end of the term to record and hand back work that was several weeks—or more—old. I looked forward to vacations or long weekends as an opportunity to catch up on my grading. I even coerced my younger sister into helping me grade papers. It felt like sorting eggs or municipal bonds—just assigning a grade against some criteria or, more likely, against the work of others in the class. I rarely knew what an A would look like until I had the whole class's grades in front of me at the end of a marking period, and I created some formula to compute grades that sorted themselves into mostly B's with some A's and a few C's and F's.

I allowed for extensions and collected late assignments from students. I gave warnings before term's end and tried to encourage students to make-up work, but I gave precious little feedback about the quality of the work in a timely fashion, and I was even less-specific in directing how to improve the work. I followed the time line established by the school and the system at large, and about one week after submitting grades, received a printout to check the accuracy of my record keeping. Students had that one week to hand in any work. Jason never stood a chance.

It wasn't that I didn't know better then or since. Through my own professional learning over the years, I learned more about giving specific feedback and considered grading in entirely new ways. I tried mastery teaching, contracts, and portfolios, developed rubrics and taught students to self-monitor and give peer feedback, and I provided detailed learning activity packages so that students would know up-front what they were expected to master over the term. Nevertheless, invariably, time was not on my side. I just could not keep up. It was only as I moved into supervision and then professional development that I had the time to experiment with the one or two classes each term. With fewer than half the number of papers requiring feedback and only one preparation for one or two sections of a course, I could respond to students in a more specific and timely manner.

I still needed to spend evenings and weekends planning and grading because other duties—including providing adult-learning experiences and feedback to teachers—also consumed my time, but I could practice what I was preaching. I could abandon the "mean" as some measure of student achievement and actually follow the practices defined most recently by Doug Reeves in his books and articles against "toxic grading."

In recent years, I taught an evening college course in secondary methods. I tried to model the kind of grading I suggested to new teachers. Students could hand in work over and over. I would provide feedback, and they could amend their efforts. Midterms and finals were extended essays where students had access to their notes, handouts, and textbooks. Homework was a log of classroom observations using professional language to label teacher practice and the observable effects on students. The only thing I could not do was extend the time for completing the course beyond a week after the semester ended. I was so exhausted by semester's end, I had to give up the class. Once again, I couldn't really keep up with the late nights, weekends, and vacation time required.

What I also found was that a number of the would-be teachers preferred to take the D or C rather than to revisit their work. Many even resented my open-ended grading policy, and resisted it in practice. Some, however, did resubmit the work using my written and verbal feedback as a guide. Two students, who got jobs as English and social studies teachers in a middle school, even reported that they tried to implement the practice of having students meet a high standard with many opportunities to complete stellar work. They also found it impossibly time-consuming.

I continue the work of broaching authentic assessment for designing student tasks and planning units of study and lessons with many educators. Unfortunately, the story doesn't have a happy ending with dozens of educators embracing a better way to assess and plan. This is not because they do not believe that students should be given the support to complete work at standards of excellence or be given specific and immediate feedback so that they can try again, but rather because there just isn't enough systemic support for what we all know is right.

The conditions under which most high school teachers in general—and English teachers in particular—work are the same as they were 30 (or more) years ago. If anything, the push for more student-contact time and less planning and assessment time is greater than conditions 30 years ago. The focus on external and more-frequent assessment has meant that teachers are less in control of assessment as feedback and more at the mercy of predictive assessments that do not predict anything. In New York City, students take multiple-choice "predictive" tests through an online assessment program for a Regents examination that is overwhelmingly extended-response in format. Teachers have less in-school time to review student work in response to teacher-constructed tasks and use it as feedback for their instruction. Moreover, the sheer number of students in high school classes organized in artificial time schedules precludes meaningful individualized study plans for students.

I see teachers going to heroic lengths to reach out to students. I see principals and supervisors trying to establish communities of practice where teachers look at student work together and assess the learning tasks given students. I talk to educators who say they are "burnt out," and we all share the standing joke: "It is vacation time. Now I can get sick"—and they do. Therefore, we all compromise. It is a lose-lose situation. We know that there is a better way, but we cannot do it. Instead, we allow a vision of all students' achieving to erode, and our students lose because we cannot make the time and space they need to excel, to learn with joy.

I often think of Jason. He took a course twice and failed it twice. He protected himself from failure by not trying, and yet, hope had not died in him. What I should have done—and wished I could have done—was give him a plan for completing, not repeating, the work to meet the standard. He had done work. He needed my attention, teaching, and guided practice to make the grade. More than 25 years later, I wonder why we still record F's instead of "Not Yet." I wonder why we cannot draw a line under the point at which a student masters the work rather than at an artificial point in time. I wonder at how little the policy makers understand that teachers are professionals who need the time and support to diagnose, prescribe for, and evaluate students' progress and achievement. The pressures on me and on all high school teachers are meted out by an artificial construct of time, number of students, and policy that meant I failed Jason and scores of others. What effect that has had on their lives I do not know. Both my failure and the unknown haunt me.

TEACHING HERE AND TEACHING THERE

Dean P. Johnson

NOTHING IS MORE appetizing to a career bureaucrat than a good, thick, hearty report. A choice cut of executive summaries, charts, and graphs—well-done and topped with sautéed statistics—will feed rapacious pen-pushers for a solid two, maybe three, hours or until the next new mandate comes along, whichever comes first.

As a school assessment coordinator, it is my job to prepare such delicacies for consumption. Starting with raw data, I carve through standardized testing results, chop them into bit-sized disaggregated pieces, and blend them into a delectable report without mincing words.

It is also my job to work with teachers to help prepare

the students for these tests with a menu of teacher professional development opportunities, lesson plans, and after-school programs.

The pressure to perform on standardized tests has never been greater. To that end, we ready the students for the exams by duplicating the conditions of testing. Among other test-preparation skills and techniques, I instruct students how to write within a limited space and a limited time on artificial topics.

Teaching writing in this way is particularly hard for me because I write. I have had essays published in newspapers all over the country, including the *Los Angeles Times, New York Times, Christian Science Monitor, Chicago Tribune,* and *Philadelphia Inquirer,* among others. I also teach creative writing at the college level, where I pursue how good writing ideas can find their own form, collaboration can polish ideas, revision is an integral part of the writing process, and sometimes, if an idea is allowed to sit and ripen, the subconscious will do the work. Those ideas contradict what I am pressured to teach: the testing cohort.

Here in New Jersey, all first-time 11th grade students must take the High School Proficiency Assessment (HSPA). The test is administered over three late winter days, one for mathematics and two for language arts. The language arts portion asks students to respond to multiple-choice and open-response questions for narrative and persuasive readings. There is also a prompt for a persuasive essay as well as a prompt for a narrative response. If students do not score in the proficient or advanced proficient ranges, they have a second opportunity to take the test in October of their senior year. Still scoring in the partially proficient range (read as do not pass), they take it again in March of their senior year along with the next cohort of first-time 11th graders. If they do not pass after three attempts, the students may not graduate with a state-endorsed diploma. Further, after three attempts the cohort is measured against the yardstick known as Adequate Yearly Progress (AYP), No Child Left Behind's narrow instrument to judge a school's value. If the current cohort's proficiency rate does not meet established benchmarks, which regularly increase and specify that by 2014 all cohorts will have to be 100 percent proficient, the school is labeled as a "school in need of improvement" or a "failing school" and is levied with sanctions, some costing the district thousands of dollars.

While it is admirable to want all students to be proficient in math, reading, and writing, a standardized test as the sole indicator greatly reduces the quality of not only learning and teaching, but professional esteem, as well.

I teach in Camden, New Jersey, a high-poverty urban setting—currently listed as the second most dangerous city in the United States. (Was ranked also as the first a few years ago.) Our students come from middle schools across the city and are generally reading two to three years below grade level when they get to us. The vast majority of our students are eligible for federal lunch programs. However, no matter what surrounding communities may say, we have good kids who endure—nay, excel—while living in societal conditions such as violence, crime, drugs, and blight that most kids their age have only experienced through cable television and video games.

All 11th graders participate in the HSPA after-school program. The students participate in two sessions, mathematics and language arts, and then are served dinner. It is not uncommon for many of our students to eat breakfast, lunch, and dinner at school. Attendance in the program is strong as we attain parent support during November parent conferences.

Our 11th grade English teacher and I meet and come up with a strategy. He spends most of his class time on reading skills, while I, during the after-school program, focus on writing.

After spending several weeks focusing on specific strategies and techniques for narrative and persuasive on-demand, timed writing, we begin practice testing, first the narrative picture prompt.

I hand out a picture. Go. Some students begin writing immediately. Most, though, sit and stare. We've talked about time management, prewriting quickly.

One student wants to tell me her idea before she begins writing. I tell her that during the test, talking is not allowed. Nevertheless, she just wants to know what

I think of it. We've been through this before. She is quite articulate and a storyteller. She and I have shared how we both like reading and writing better than math and science. She once told me her idea for a short story she plans on writing about a young girl who befriends an angel. We then talked of magical realism, and I promised to bring her in a short story by Gabriel Garcia Marquez that I know she will enjoy. This test is not about all that, though. I tell her to write the narrative, and I'll tell her what I think of it afterward.

Another student asks how to spell a word. She is a student whose parents speak little English. She herself was born in Camden and has only been to Puerto Rico two or three times visiting relatives. The only times she speaks English is when she is at school. She knows when a word doesn't look right, when she is spelling a word how she hears it in her mind's ear. She is not an ESL student; she speaks English too well. It's just that she's so accustomed to the Spanish that sometimes the English throws her. I remind them that a teacher is not allowed to help with spelling or anything else during the test and remind them that no reference materials, such as a dictionary or thesaurus, are permitted. I picture my own writing space at home with these aids at arm's reach.

When time is called, I collect the papers.

I read over the students' stories. Several are incomplete. I speak with one student about managing her time. She nods, says she knows, and then tells me how the story will end. It's a good idea, too, but I know she won't finish it on her own because this is test prep. My stomach pangs, and I am frustrated at the lost opportunity for development. Other students complain that they didn't know what certain things were in the picture. Still others say it's hard for them because they start to second-guess every idea they have, and then they keep thinking about the clock ticking away.

A student hands in a paper that is a budding garden of good ideas but peppered with squashed-out words, phrases, and sentences; long arrows that plow through lines; and more carets than you can shake a second thought at. He is a student who has become disaffected with school. He has been known to be disruptive in a class and asks a lot of off-topic yet seemingly logical questions like: "Wouldn't it be better if I wrote about something I really cared about?" He is pleasant, insightful, and remains focused when I work with him one-on-one. In group settings, he seeks out, and often attains, the class's attention.

His composition is difficult to read. Between the cross-outs and scribbled additions, it is easy to lose your place. I fear that a test grader, one hired as temporary help to read thousands of essays and quickly deem them proficient or not, may be negatively influenced by this. I know graders won't take too much time on any one response, so I talk to the student about making fewer cross-outs. I can't believe I hear myself essentially telling him not to revise during the test. I think about my college class in which I dedicate at least two two-and-a-half-hour classes to workshopping and revising writing. I tell the students that in revision comes brilliance. My stomach pangs again. He wants to rewrite it, and I want him to. However, the time has expired. Sure, I'll look over it with him tomorrow, but tomorrow will bring a new topic and a reset timer.

The persuasive essay topics generally ask the students to imagine that something has happened at their school that has become a controversial issue. The students are to write a letter agreeing or disagreeing with the issue.

"Can't we decide what to write about?" students always ask me. They often complain they cannot relate to the topics. They say it would be a lot easier for them to write about something they know, something they actually care about. Yes, I say. I understand. My college students write about things they know, things they care about. I write about things I know, things I care about. You can, too, I tell them, but not right now. Now we practice formulaic writing based on the holistic scoring rubric. The rubric tells us what the readers are looking for, so we make sure these things are evident in the writing. However, this is only one type of writing, one genre of writing, I tell them again.

I seem to be constantly reminding the high school students that I am teaching them a particular genre of writing, that is, on-demand, timed writing. Maybe that is simply a rationalization on my part to ease my pangs, my tug-of-war within. If I give this writing I am pressured to teach its own name, its own category, I can say it's one small part of many types of writing. Nevertheless, I know it's not. It is not how writers write, but it is how they can pass a test, and it is how we show the ravenous gourmands governing public education how one particular measurable objective, from which an entire school will be judged, can be met.

My high school is successful. Our state test scores are good. We make Adequate Yearly Progress. We have taught our students how to achieve within the limited scope of standardized writing, and I am glad for that. However, I fear that I have left my students editorially malnourished, and I am left with an empty, unsatisfied feeling in the pit of my gut.

Fortunately, I am able to supplement my pedagogical diet with a weekly dose of university teaching.

One of the first activities I do with my university creative writing class each semester is an exploration of each student's writing history and process. Prompted by a few memory exercises and leading questions, the class examines why and how we write. My own process varies from piece to piece, but essentially, I'll rapidly jot down ideas related to a topic that has caught my interest. I'll write a draft for a couple of hours and then let it sit until the next day when I read it over and inevitably delete two-thirds. This process continues for several days until the piece has reached a recognizable form. From that point, I'll read it to my wife, editing out things that just don't sound right as I go along. Then I go back and revise again.

My high school students will have an hour to write a persuasive essay and a half hour to write a narrative prompted by a picture. There is little time for process in mandated standardized testing.

The pictures I use with my high school students I know can be put to better use than a 30-minute timed writing prompt. Pictures can be a richly effective springboard for strong, authentic writing.

One activity I do with my college students helps them recall and refine a memory. I bring in a stack of old magazines and ask the class to peruse them until they find a picture that reminds them of a past event. The class is then paired up and each student, in turn, tells his or her partner the story of the remembered event. After about five minutes, I hand out a paper with a list of questions meant to clarify the memory: What other people were with you? What happened right before/after the event? What was around you when this was taking place? What is it about the picture that reminded you of the experience? How did the event make you feel? How does remembering it now make you feel?

After a few more minutes of paired discussion, the students then write out the story of their memory. The writing usually takes about 10 to 15 minutes. The students then read what they have written.

When the readings are through, we discuss the process. We talk about how stimulating the senses can help recall, like the smells of foods or the sound of songs. We further discuss how talking through the memory and asking questions can help elucidate it so that we have the image clearly in front of us as we start to write.

Another activity I do with my creative writing class is to use pictures to teach characterization. I hand out several different pictures of faces. Students then work on giving personalities to these faces: names, unique traits, how they walk, speak, and laugh. We give the faces belongings, objects that reflect who they are. We give them joy, aspirations, disappointments, and failures. We give them voice by having them tell us what compels them to act. We ask them questions. We put them in various situations. In the end, the students have created a character with a distinctive voice and complex personality.

This process—the exercises, discussions, and collaborations—can take the whole two and a half hours of class. It's time well spent. In the environment of mandated state testing, however, it seems one cannot afford such frivolous spending.

As long as bureaucrats crave the fast food of assessments, standardized testing will continue to clog the arteries of authentic experience, genuine writing, satisfying teaching, and quality education for those students I hunger to teach.

EYES IN THE BACK OF HER HEAD

Viviane Verstandig

BEFORE 2001, MOST elementary school teachers in New York tried to avoid teaching the fourth grade. Grade 4 was the pressure point; in grade 4 New York State English language arts and mathematics tests were administered. Scores were scrutinized, publicized in the newspapers, and could make or break a teacher's professional reputation. Students who did not meet benchmark levels were threatened with retention and dispatched to summer school. Teachers were informally evaluated on how well their classes performed. The principal would demand an explanation if students performed poorly; if the students did well, the teacher was "condemned" to teach the fourth grade for eternity, as a principal would never want to change a successful program. Witnessing the pressure of the fourth grade, teachers with seniority would consistently opt for a teaching assignment in any other grade.

However, all of that changed with the passage of the 2001 No Child Left Behind Act, which instituted standardized testing in third through eighth grade in English language arts and mathematics. All teachers would find themselves under the harsh glare of the testing spotlight. Teachers of the primary grades thought that they were safe in the shadows of their upper-grade counterparts, but it wasn't long before a complex assessment program in New York City would be instituted for measuring achievement in literacy in the youngest of age groups, kindergarten to second grade.

New York City adopted the Early Childhood Literacy Assessment (ECLAS-2) six years ago. The purpose is for the teacher to be able to gather a child's literacy development as he or she moves from kindergarten to third grade. The data in the assessment follows each student as he or she moves from grade to grade. Benchmark levels can be used for promotional criteria.

The assessment is given in the fall and in the spring, with the exception of kindergarten students who take the initial assessment in January. Back in 2007, another change was implemented when the Department of Education concluded that the majority of kindergartners needed some literacy instruction before they could be tested.

Now, when first grade teacher Amanda Wilson (not her real name) starts the job of tackling all the different parts to ECLAS-2, she knows that of the four group activity assessments, the spelling and the vocabulary tests are the easiest to manage. She plans to administer the group activities when all of her students are present, eliminating the time factor in giving make ups. After giving the tests, Amanda collects the answer sheets, grades them, and records the scores in each student's individual ECLAS-2 booklet.

The palpable stress of administering ECLAS-2 begins when Amanda has to complete the six individual activities with each one of her students. Each activity outlines benchmark levels that students must meet at each grade in the fall term and spring term to demonstrate proficiency. In order to provide an optimal testing environment for each one of her students, Amanda tries to conduct the assessments in a "quiet" location in her first grade classroom. The assessments are done during independent work time in readers' workshop, and she purposefully finds an area that is slightly removed from the rest of the children.

Amanda asks six-year-old Marcus to one corner of the classroom. She leans in to listen to Marcus attempting to read, but she grows uneasy. She sees through the eyes in the back of her head that Vincent has not begun reading, and Tiffany and Kathy are talking and swinging their feet trying to tag each other. Amanda doesn't want to interrupt Marcus while he is reading aloud. She wants to document his miscues and execute a careful and correct assessment, but her inner teacher voice is instructing her to refocus Tiffany and Kathy and she is distracted. Meanwhile, Louis slowly approaches and whines, "Miss Wilson, I have a stomachache. I feel hot." Amanda interrupts Marcus's reading, touches Louis's forehead, and confirms he feels feverish. She asks Sahar to accompany Louis to the nurse, writing a note explaining the reason for the visit. Amanda apologizes to Marcus, and asks him to continue reading aloud. When Marcus finishes reading the text, Amanda announces to the class that it is now "partner time." She compliments her class for working diligently, refocuses the students who have misbehaved, and waits for the partners to settle in so she can resume Marcus's assessment. Marcus scores well and attains mastery, which means Amanda must test him on the next level. Due to the lack of time, she will continue the following day.

For approximately three weeks during ECLAS-2 assessments, which she does twice a year, Amanda is not able to offer effective reading instruction. Following her mini-lesson demonstration, she will be unable to conduct individual conferences or provide small group instruction. The share portion of the workshop is compromised during the assessment period, as Amanda is busy focusing on one student and is not sure which of her other students she can call on to model her mini-lesson demonstration correctly. She knows that effective pedagogy requires ongoing observation of her students, offering constructive and instructive feedback, and planning the students' next steps. She feels frustrated and rushes to finish all the assessments so that proper classroom instruction may resume.

Testing the students individually, without the rest of the class present is the preferred assessment environment. Amanda often tries to administer the assessment during her preparation periods, the time in the day she needs to prepare for other instructional activities. When Amanda administers an individualized activity to one of her first graders, she continues until the mastery level is determined. For instance, in the sight-word activity, there are 135 words a student reads. The activity concludes when the child has made five consecutive errors. A first grade benchmark for the spring term is being able to read 50 of the 135 words. A student who has an advanced sight vocabulary may read 100 out of 135 words; that student would be at the benchmark level for the spring term of second grade.

Amanda will spend between 10 and 30 minutes administering each activity to her energetic first graders. She'll spend more time on her advanced readers; she'll have to continue to challenge her first grader until she can determine his or her appropriate level. The reading accuracy and comprehension is a running record, with both oral and silent reading of a book, followed by comprehension questions. Amanda documents each student's miscues, self-corrections, and responses to comprehension questions in their individual booklets. If a child reads a selection accurately and comprehends the text, another book at a more difficult level must be given.

Upon completing ECLAS-2 assessments for an entire class, teachers like Amanda pay the most attention to the reading accuracy and comprehension activities, which forms a running record. A running record helps teachers determine students' independent and instructional reading levels, but it is also important for teachers to analyze what system the child uses to read—and this takes more time. When students are learning how to read, they use three cueing systems interchangeably. The systems they use are: semantic word meaning (does the word make sense in a particular sentence?), syntactic sentence structure (are the words in the sentence grammatically correct—does it sound right?), and the grapho-phonic cueing system (are the sound-symbol relationships correct—does it look right?). It is essential that teachers analyze the student's miscues to determine possible trends and a reliance on one or two of the systems instead of employing all three. Once the teacher analyzes the miscues, an individualized instructional plan can be implemented noting which reading strategies the student uses with automaticity and which ones require further teaching.

When Amanda completes the assessment, she has documented the reading patterns of each of her 22 students. However, sifting through the nine separate activities, in each of these booklets is an overwhelming task. The booklets often sit in her closet and remain untouched until the next testing window.

Two years ago, the Department of Education provided several schools with an experimental trial program of using PDAs for ECLAS-2. Our school participated in the program. The teachers could record all data from the ECLAS onto a Palm Pilot without ever needing paper or pencil. The teachers liked the ease of recording the data. Undoubtedly, the best part about using the Palm Pilots was the ability to synchronize the data into specialized software. The information could be used immediately for instructional purposes, as students could be grouped by their strengths and weaknesses for each individual activity. Finally, teachers were able to use the data efficiently through the use of technology. Accumulating huge amounts of information does not necessarily lead to better instruction if teachers lack the ability or time to implement it properly.

In the fall of 2008, the Department of Education added another assessment that schools could use in addition to ECLAS-2: the Dynamic Indicators of Basic Early Literacy Skills (DIBELS). The advantage of using DIBELS is the ability to assess each individual student within 10 minutes. However, there is tremendous controversy on the instructional benefits of using DIBELS, as it promotes reading with speed and fluency without encouraging the use of comprehension skills and strategies. Amanda and her colleagues were frustrated with the data from DIBELS, as the results indicated the students were not demonstrating literacy growth while the teachers were seeing evidence of learning through class work and their observations. If a student was not able to read quickly, the student did not meet the DIBELS benchmark.

When teachers do not see the value or use the information from the assessments, it becomes frustrating, as it infringes upon their valuable instructional time. ECLAS-2 has many activities that teachers must administer but do not use for planning daily instruction. For example, ECLAS-2 contains a vocabulary test in the Reading and Oral Expression strand. The vocabulary test is one of the group activities that teachers read to the students as they follow along. The teacher reads a sentence and the students must identify a synonym for a particular word. The ECLAS instructions state that if a student fails to meet the specific grade benchmark level, the teacher must analyze the student's sight words, reading accuracy, oral expression, and writing expression to determine if he or she requires further vocabulary instruction.

I have never seen teachers analyze the data from the vocabulary assessment because they already know which of their students have limited oral language. Teachers incorporate vocabulary instruction throughout the day, embedding it in their read-alouds and classroom discussions. Nevertheless, the vocabulary activity is part of the assessment and teachers must score the test and enter the data.

In 2008, the same year that they introduced DIBELS, the Department of Education launched a pilot program to test kindergarten students with a 60–90 minute paper and pencil standardized assessment. Does the Department of Education believe that only through more testing, students will demonstrate greater academic growth and proficiency? Early childhood experts have claimed over the past 15 years that four- and five-year-olds need time for imaginative play, as it develops both their academic and social skills. With the tremendous emphasis on test scores, less and less time can be devoted to play. What happened to the relaxed and laid-back atmosphere of kindergarten? When the kindergarten teachers in my school were upset that play time was gradually being eliminated because of all the academic pressures, my principal assured the teachers that their schedules had to include time for play every day. The kindergarten classrooms continue to have a kitchen center, supermarket corner, and block area for building and dramatic play. Unfortunately, in some schools those areas no longer exist; they only have reading, writing, and math centers.

As kindergarten has become an academically

rigorous grade, Amanda, and other first grade teachers, faces a dilemma when a child, who has never attended school, enters their classrooms. (New York and many other states offer kindergarten programs, but attendance is not mandatory.) How will they support this new student who is unable to identify the letters of the alphabet or write his or her name? The student struggles and tries to keep up with the first grade curriculum while his or her peers have already attained a year of literacy instruction.

As data, data, data has been the new buzzwords of the new millennium, it is imperative that the stakeholders in the educational community remember that we are working with students who do not all develop at the same rate and time. Student achievement will not increase from constant assessments. Teachers should focus on the reason why they entered this profession: to make a difference in the lives of children, which is reflected in their faces, not solely in their test scores.

CLEAR EXPECTATIONS

Diana Garcia

FOR THE LAST 11 years, I have taught at an East Austin, Texas, school in a bilingual fourth grade classroom. Hispanic children make up 87 percent of our population, with 49 percent being English language learners (ELLs). African Americans comprise 11 percent, and Anglo children make up 1 percent. Ninety-five percent of our students receive free or reduced price lunch.

In the years I've been there, our school has gone through seven different principals, so we've had little consistency or strong leadership to work toward some vision or plan for improvement. Sure, each year we start off with the Campus Improvement Plan, but each principal has had a different view, different methods of communicating with staff, different programs, and so far, no one principal has stayed with the school long enough to make a difference. On GreatSchools.net, we are rated a 2, on a scale of 1 to 10, with 10 being ideal. The ratings are based on how well students do on standardized tests. Tests—I hate them! But first, a few vignettes…

The latest principal seems a tad stressed when informing us that "people from Central Offices will be doing walk-throughs." A few days before the slated visit, she and the assistant principal walk diligently through all classrooms. What learning charts and expectations are displayed? Are all teams aligned? Is student work up? Is each class visitor-from-Central-worthy?!

My daily class schedule, posted outside my class, does not meet expected standards because it does not explicitly state each component of the day. The assistant principal takes it, and says she will type it up for me. Later, I get a new schedule that tells me exactly what I should teach and when. My old schedule said: "Language Arts 8:00–10:30." The new and improved schedule says: "Read Aloud/Shared Reading 8:00–8:30, Guided Reading Groups, 8:30–9:30," and so forth, with each subject perfectly dissected and given a time slot. Each day, I have from 10:30 AM until 10:40 AM to teach the math "problem of the day."

In my classroom, I had "accountable talk" sentence strips up on the wall. These are sentence starters for students, so that if I ask them a question, they can look at the "accountable talk" stubs and choose one: "I agree because...," "I have a connection to...," "May I get more information about..."

Yes, these handy sentence starters were up, along with clear expectations (a list of behaviors expected and consequences if specific behaviors were not in place), and a crisp new daily schedule. The visitors from Central seemed pleased as they breezed into our class rooms for three to five minutes. They viewed the test-taking strategies charts up on all the classrooms, and apparently decided that real learning was going on that day! How simple!

Moreover, to make sure this real learning happens at our school, each grade level teacher team gets to go to two-to-three-hour meetings where we learn, re-learn, and revisit test-taking strategies. That way we are all on the same page and have clear expectations. We watch a literacy coach model, for the 999th time, on how to show students step-by-step test strategies. We get this every year, and somehow we are still rated a 2!

During one meeting, our principal asked the fourth grade teachers, we who are entrusted with getting our students prepared for the writing test, if we knew the difference between revision and editing. Hmmm, let me see.... They might have mentioned something about that in the National Writing Program I went through, or in some of the massive writing training I have had for the last 11 years, but I felt better knowing my principal cared enough to check whether her team of fourth grade teachers were morons or not, and that we all now had clear expectations.

I love read-aloud time, when I choose a classic from children's literature to share with my students, but now read-aloud time has become test-crunch time! All fourth grade teachers have been told read-aloud must last 15 to 20 minutes, with each passage read followed by some test-like question. These are called "TAKS stems," and we have been given two binders full of stems—lest we are unable to think on our own. TAKS stands for "tests are killing students!!!" That all important No Creativity Left Behind law says all teachers in Texas have to give the Texas Assessment of Knowledge and Skills (TAKS), and it doesn't matter if it kills teachers or students, (metaphorically speaking, of course), because we have to prove how accountable we are. So now on Wednesdays and Thursdays we no longer have time for beautiful read-alouds because we have to model testing strategies with the dry and boring passages sent to us from Central Offices: and on Fridays, the students are given weekly tests to see if they are using their strategies.

At least on Mondays and Tuesdays, I still have those precious 15 to 20 minutes to read from *The Secret Garden*. When I stop reading, my students often cry out, "No!!!! What's going to happen? Read some more!"

Teachers get a 30-minute duty-free lunch break, but I choose to let my students eat with me almost every day. We get to listen to music or watch movies with social justice themes like *Rabbit-Proof Fence, Children of Paradise,* or *The Story of Ruby Bridges.* If I leave them in the cafeteria, the monitors nag at them the whole time, "No talking! No talking!"

I feel like our time together during lunch is our own "secret garden," a time to enjoy each other's company without worrying about tests, charts, accountable talk, and the constant negative mantra that runs through our school, the hissing, snarling sound of "Get busy! Work! Work! Get busy!"

What happens to the souls of administrators and some teachers? Do they *really not* remember what it felt like to be a child? Were they seriously working, working, working all the time as children?! Were they *always on task?!*

Honestly, even though I am an adult, I still feel joy, passion, and goofiness. I can still relate to children, and that's part of the reason I chose a teaching career. Also, I wanted to inspire students to love literature, to love thinking, to ask questions, to challenge the history books, to learn the importance of empathy and kindness, to learn how to problem-solve, and to learn how to become agents of change. It's difficult, though, and frustrating, when my principal and assistant principal do constant walk-throughs to see if I am following directives to focus mainly on getting these students prepared to take one test, one day of the school year. In addition, I am given inauthentic passages and resources to use—and oodles of test-taking strategies and clear expectations—but all I'm registering these days is that I am not trusted enough, not respected enough to be allowed to use or to voice my teaching methods, vision, or own experiences as a learner and teacher. Moreover, hardly anyone listens to the voices of the children, their dreams, fears, hopes, and desires.

Nevertheless, we have our secret moments, the magical borders we create when we are "off task," when I allow my students to pursue their own interests because I believe that in a democratic society children should have time for their own interests. Like when my Spanish-speaking students teach their English-speaking buddies a few phrases in Spanish and J., who knows very little Spanish, comes up to me beaming and asks, *"Que estas hacienda?"*

We celebrate small victories. Each morning we start off by giving compliments to each other. The students know when someone needs a "warm fuzzy." S., the hyperactive, sometimes mean girl, has been trying her best to be kinder and calmer. It does not go unnoticed as L. shares, "I gave a compliment to S. She helped me with my math yesterday, and she was not being hyper!"

Sometimes we sing silly songs about our dendrites or about tea-sipping penguins, and we laugh at corny jokes, and we almost forget about all the tests that loom over us, which dictate so much of our curriculum. As much as I can, I try to convey to my students via the books, stories, and poems I use in my class, via the writing exercises I have them do, the group projects we work on, and the choices I offer them, that life is so much more complicated, painful, wondrous, and amazing than a multiple-choice test.

For now, the law of the land is NCLB and the need for accountability. In keeping with this law, please answer the following questions based on TAKS stems so you may see if you understood what you just read.

The author of this piece probably wrote this essay because

A. she loves standardized tests.
B. she wants to praise her principal and school district.
C. she's insane.
D. she might be feeling the pressures of teaching.

It is reasonable to infer that the author of this piece will likely

A. need to be looking for a new career soon.
B. get voted Teacher of the Year.
C. not get a letter of recommendation from her principal.
D. be running away to join a circus.

Which of the following can cause feelings of frustration and pressure?

A. An excellent salary

B. Receiving respect
C. Being supplied with lots of support and resources
D. Clear expectations that your students' low-performing TAKS scores will be shared with everyone at a faculty meeting

FALSE STARTS AND FAILURES:

IN SEARCH OF A NEW MODEL FOR INTEGRATING TECHNOLOGY INTO THE CLASSROOM

Fred Hass

I REMEMBER ONE of my first interviews for a teaching position. I sat across from a small team of interviewers that included the principal. One of the questions they asked me was how would I use technology in the classroom. It struck me as an odd question, at the time, because even a pencil is technology, but I knew what they meant. The real question was "How would I use computers?" The train of technology integration (read: computers and the Internet) had already left the station—and it was clear that nearly every administrator was chasing behind trying to jump aboard, regardless of consequence.

This was in the beginning of 2004; I was about to receive my teaching certification after nearly a decade since graduating college. In that time, I had worked in the education technology industry as a consultant, specializing in teacher training and streaming video integration. Remember, this was pre-YouTube, and the only way to get quality video that was better than a postage stamp of pixelated, stuttering images was to run it over a network. The trouble was that all of these spectacular new innovations were extremely expensive and not terribly reliable. Simply rolling out computers, which at that time cost over $2,000 a box, to every classroom presented a host of technical problems, especially in schools not exactly built to accommodate these new data networks. So much has changed in such a short time. Now that prices have fallen and a host of Internet devices are readily available, there is even more pressure on schools to integrate technology into the classroom. Yet genuine success continues to be haphazard, especially in content areas.

What is amazing and frustrating to me is how few really identify this in the grand push for technology integration in the classroom. Rare is the decision maker that has the depth of vision and breadth of understanding to recognize how powerful and disruptive technology initiatives can be. Rather, a blind mantra of it's-the-way-of-the-future continues to be mouthed year after year, and administrators and computer companies continue to cut deals to get more machines in a classroom, even in individual students' hands. In most cases, this is the by-product of a creeping business model mind-set infecting education. However, education and industry have some profound differences in technology adoption and integration. That model simply does not work.

Businesses continue to be early adopters of technology, be it computers or gadgets, because there is a premium on efficiency. Anything that will make workers faster and more productive is a key factor in driving profitability. Plus, a business can recover from failed technology initiatives with much greater ease, if for no other reason than that they can drive sales, make more money, and soften the financial costs associated with the failure. A business leader can decide that his or her whole company is going to use a certain product, and later discover it does not provide an important feature that has become newly critical for success. Instead, the same person can force the switch to another product, and everyone will fall in line and work through all the kinks and problems. (They want to keep their jobs, after all.) There is also an expectation that this kind of thing will happen, and does routinely, in the business world. Everyone generally understands that technology

can and does fail. In addition, with rare exceptions, a
glitch that can be remedied within a few hours is an
inconvenience not a calamity. Moreover, in large businesses, the glitch is usually being handled by a sizable
team of highly trained, well-paid, professional support
staff. Almost none of the factors mentioned here reflect
the world of education.

Education, K–12, traditionally has not been able to
afford being early adopters due to the price and pain.
Furthermore, there is no primary profit motive for
a public school, which generally even lacks accounts
receivable functionality. Moreover, learning is not necessarily a process best measured by efficiency. If learning
is education's chief concern, we have to recognize the
fits and starts involved in the process for a student and
teacher alike. It is an inherently inefficient process, yet
that stops few from forcing more elements and competing factors, including new and innovative computer use,
into the time allotted for learning.

Failed technology initiatives for schools are pro-
foundly costly and wasteful, because schools have more
limited resources than industry. While a business executive might be sent packing, an administrator who makes
a decision such as the one previously highlighted almost
assuredly finds himself looking for new employment.
The stakes are higher when there is little means for miti-
gating an ultimately poor decision with greater business
growth. Moreover, less understanding is shown when

public money is ill spent, and the wrath of blame mounts with greater weight.

Another factor is that businesses deal with different workforce issues. Business employees that refuse to fall in line, adopt a new solution, and persevere through all of the kinks are undoubtedly told to gather their things and leave. The public education system is filled with a large body of teachers that have been working in classrooms successfully with limited computer use, or none at all, for some time. Therefore, firing a teacher because he or she will not adopt a new and improved technology initiative of any kind is nearly impossible, apart from being impractical. Beyond that, how does a school know without the certainty of regular and direct observation whether a teacher has adopted the new effort? What is the metric? In business, profit drives everything and is the easiest of metrics. The company is in the red or the black. There is no single metric that so simply determines the failure or success of a school on any level, let alone the integration of technology. Beyond that, I am reminded of my time training teachers, when a common remark was, "How do I turn the thing off?"

Schools also generally have limited resources when it comes to ongoing support and help desk operations. Most teachers are lucky to have one person that addresses the problems of the whole school—schools with dozens, if not hundreds, of computers. This becomes a profound threat to a positive initial experience and to as well as ensuring that any experience will continue along positive lines. Schools rarely pay their support staff the kind of money that the same individuals can get working in industry. As a result, good candidates are harder to come by and more difficult to retain. Rare is the school that I have seen, before becoming a teacher or since, that manages the support issue exceptionally well.

Ultimately, what many fail to realize is that technological breakdowns and glitches in a classroom are an invitation for chaos. A teacher standing in front of a classroom of kids, most of whom think they know more about computers than the teacher does, regardless of whether that is, truth or not, is extraordinarily vulnerable. When things go wrong and the teacher cannot easily address the issue, they very quickly begin to lose credibility with the students. This is particularly true during beginnings—the beginning of classes, terms, or units—when a teacher is most likely to use a computer for presentation purposes in the first place. This is an especially acute problem for newly certified teachers, most of whom have neither the experience nor the ability to adjust quickly to the unexpected mechanical failure. Yet more than anything, it becomes an instant distraction for the teacher and is a situation that is rife with classroom management problems. As the teacher tries to address the problem, students sit idly and are given the opportunity to misbehave. In addition, the timing of the class is disrupted, which is another potential problem for the teacher in managing students. None of these scenarios are good for the teacher's credibility with the students.

I am reminded of a recent experience I had with an honors English class deeply invested in an international, multischool technology project. Students worked in teams with students in other classrooms around the world to develop Wiki pages, as well as making their own individual short videos about how the future of education should be. This was precisely the kind of immersive technology integration experience touted as the pathway to 21st-century skills. I knew going into the project that there was a host of potential problems that I could anticipate and prepare the class for accordingly. However, I also knew that there would be issues that I could in no way anticipate, and I braced myself for them. Further complicating things was a deadline that I could not control because we were participating in something much larger than our class. Clearly, the scale and scope of this project would make many a teacher pause.

I did the best I could to prepare the students, imploring them to maintain their focus on the task no matter what problems came our way. Yet the number of technical issues that arose could have been catastrophic in terms of managing a class. The school's resources were at an all-time premium. Hardware was limited and many computers failed at critical moments. Software simply did not work or needed enhancements and updates to function. Access to necessary online resources was initially limited or unavailable. All of these complications emerged in addition to the complexities of actually teaching any of the associated content. Simply, the number of people revolving in and out of the classroom alone revealed the degree of potential distraction. It required extraordinary patience and perseverance on the part of the students.

During the run of the project, I benefitted from no less than seven additional people who were there to help solve problems, as we closed in on the deadline. The district technology coordinator was in my classroom every day of the project, and needed to be. She essentially had to act as an advocate for the kinds of rights and permissions clearance needed to add necessary software and so much more. Our school's help desk technician was a regular fixture when the students began editing their videos, managing all manner of software and video codec problems, as well as storage issues. Our media specialist assisted with distribution and management of all necessary audio and video equipment. A network administrator was virtually on call the whole time for any number of related bottlenecks and bandwidth problems. By the end, the film and television teacher was on hand, with two 12th grade assistants, to assist me and the technology coordinator in an all-hands-on-deck drive to get each student's video to a final cut, compressed, and uploaded to the appropriate destination in time to be judged by panels of international educator judges.

Granted this is an extreme example but an instructive one. The experience, with its 21st-century skills and technology integration exactly the kind that administrators seek from teachers. Nevertheless, all of the support listed was necessary to be successful within the time and technological constraints, even with a class of 22 of the best and brightest ninth graders in the school. I simply could not have accomplished the deceptively complicated undertaking without that level of technical assistance. There were far too many problems that I did not have the permission to solve or may not have had quick and easy solutions for. Regardless, they continually ate away at actual instructional time. More to the point, the amount of time and effort required to solve many of the problems or arrange for solutions sapped nearly all the time I had during the day, while I was not committed to teaching that class or others. Still, what schools are ready to handle those kinds of integration pains? Could they provide a level of support even close to what was needed? How many schools would be willing to make that kind of commitment? How many teachers would have called it quits before even starting?

Over time, some things have changed, such as failures becoming less expensive monetarily. More new teachers enter the profession every year that are adept computer users, have grown up with the Internet, and can integrate technological elements more easily into their teaching, if the resources are available. Yet the most critical truism that endures is this: In education, the success of any technology initiative involving teachers in classrooms is entirely predicated on a positive and easy initial user experience. In almost all cases I have observed as a teacher or consultant, it is absolutely critical that each teacher's first time using a new technology tool be a good one. If there are any problems when that teacher first attempts to use hardware or software, that initiative will be dead on arrival. Technology integration can be successful and should be part of future planning, but an understanding of this technology is required.

Why, Why, Why?

Maureen Picard Robins

Each year after commencement exercises, the eighth grade graduates return to school for one more celebration: the annual Junior High School picnic, a full day of outdoor fun, complete with DJ, hula hoops, barbeque, and leisure time to sign yearbooks and reminisce. This year, to save money, my principal is (wo)manning the grill along with another assistant principal. She's given up on the goodie bags she had us put together last time for the graduates, but the spirit of celebration and inventiveness remains. The picnic, conceived several years ago as a ploy to lure graduates back to school one more day and protect our attendance data, has become a right of passage and an easy target for typical adolescent love and scorn.

Not everyone is invited to the picnic, however. Eighth graders must have passed all four core subjects to be able to participate. Those students who failed one or more core subjects were sequestered in a classroom to do work and view a film. This removal generates serious junior high buzz—even though it affected only a few students. Some teachers take secret pleasure in the sequestering of these students. These kids were a handful and had drained a the lion's share of our goodwill and our preparatory time (phoning parents, writing up student removal forms, documenting their bad behavior). They were the proverbial "squeaky wheel," seeking negative attention from other classmates and from us. Out of a class of nearly 400 students, less than $1/10$ were scheduled to attend summer school for failing one or more classes. One students was scheduled to be held over. On that day, almost all of the 34 students appeared. Many of them said their parents made them come to school as punishment.

Because our school is located within one of the five boroughs of New York City, the picnic does not unfold on a grassy acre beside a baseball diamond. Our school, built 50 years ago to last an eternity, rests adjacent to an urban, public playground, an asphalt polygon enclosed by an 18 foot tall chain-link fence. Basketball hoops line the periphery, and two handball courts are positioned at the farthest section of the school yard. Handball is a game where players slap a pink ball against a six to eight foot tall concrete wall. Hands are used the way racquets are used in the game of squash.

Half an hour into the picnic, the custodians have loaded two ice-filled metal washtubs with bottled water and soda, and parent volunteers are mixing greens for salad. Heat shimmers above the grills as the coals transform from black blocks to glowing embers. Students have begun trickling out of the school building and into the yard. They wander in the spring sunshine as if blinded initially by the natural light—or they are stunned by the idea that their days at junior high are truly over. My principal radios me on the walkie-talkie: four boys, obviously truant, are playing handball and need to be asked to leave.

Indeed there are four teenage boys—two from another neighborhood school and two of my eighth graders, Fred, and his best friend, Bill, who has been late to school 45 out of 180 days. Vincent is one child being left behind. I think I know them well. I know their scores and their report card grades. I know their test history and where they live. I have spoken to their parents. I have encouraged them through the year. I have given them detention for lateness. I have let them do their homework in my office. They have listened to me patiently knowing that I will eventually stop talking and go away.

I ask two of the boys to go home and suggest to our boys that they go into the building through the front door. Three of them stand outside the fence negotiating something with each other, leaving Vincent behind to swat a ball around.

"Vincent," I say, "you have to leave or go into the school."

Vincent kneels briefly on one knee to tie his neon orange shoelaces, and then rises to slap the pink ball.

"I don't have to go anywhere," Vincent says.

I am surprised at Vincent's response. He is angry, hostile. My thoughts move quickly, nonreflectively. *I've never seen him this way.*

I shout at Vincent.

Clearly, as Leslie A. Hart explains in his book *Human Brain and Human Learning,* both Vincent and I have "downshifted." Hart explains that "when the individual detects *threat* in an immediate situation, full use of the great new cerebral brain is suspended, and faster-acting, simpler brain resources take larger roles." We are in "reptilian brain," a nondiscriminating part of our think-organ that allows for no negotiation, only anger, fear, fight, or flight.

Vincent's ready for fight, but I'm fairly certain he's frightened, too. Ditto for me.

Word that the boys refuse to leave has reached my principal, who, earlier, had shown her softer side to several latecomers. She directs another assistant principal to assist me and as he walks my, way he says two things on the walkie-talkie so that Vincent can hear: tell Vincent we are going to call the truant officers if he doesn't leave the school yard and go into the school building, and we will be phoning his parents to come pick him up.

Here is the child who refuses to be left behind. He wants to participate with his peers but outside the circle of the mainstream eighth grade community. Vincent can't connect that his desire to be an outsider runs contrary to the mayor's initiative of school accountability and the federal government's No Child Left Behind legislation. No matter how much natural intelligence Vincent may possess, he is not self aware in his interactions with others. In the classroom he hasn't demonstrated any type of curiosity. His teachers have observed him throughout the year as uninvolved, "a distraction to others," and someone who does not do his homework or assignments.

Nevertheless, Vincent refuses to leave the playground, digging his metaphorical heals into the asphalt, declaring to us that this is *his* playground, his territory. In fact, many students who choose to cut out on their extended day remediation activities come straight here to the handball courts. They come to the edge of the yard, testing their limits, looking back to see what teachers and deans are watching.

Eventually, the truant officer arrives, and Harry and Vincent are escorted back into the building to join the other sequestered eighth graders.

We wait for Vincent's parents who never appear.

In December, six months prior to the June picnic,

I had an experience with my 14-year-old daughter that had a profound impact on me as a middle school educator. When she was a baby, she had an organ transplant. She is followed by her local pediatric specialist, but annually she visits her surgeon. When we arrived for her annual exam, the transplant team was all assembled, including the hospital social worker. I knew they were going to be happy to see her, but I wondered why so many people were in the room.

"So," the transplant coordinator began, "you're 14. This is the time when we begin to prepare for that day when you transition from a children's facility to an adult transplant hospital." This is something my daughter is not anxious to do. She turned to my daughter and asked a simple set of questions: *Do you know what happened to you? Why you had a transplant?* She went on when my daughter answered all the questions correctly: *How do you know when you're sick? When you are sick do you know what to do? Do you know when you need to call a doctor? Do you know how to get your medicine?*

The transplant team's data suggested that middle school teenagers (in my daughter's case, first year of high school) inhabited a middle ground. They usually need to be transitioned to adult facilities that don't call home if you miss an appointment and don't or check on your laboratory results periodically to make sure there were lab tests at the appropriate intervals. The pediatric team envisions their children off at college without parental figures reminding teens to take their antirejection medication.

The parallels to my own conferences with adolescents were unmistakable. Would high schools keep track of the students as we do? Do high schools and colleges contact parents as often as we do? The transplant team was guided by its own data about transitioning children through a medical continuum; middle schools need to acquire data that examines the transition from elementary school to high school. We should be assessing students based on whether or not they know how to do a given project or assignment. We should be asking: *Do you know when you are failing? Do you know what to do if you are failing? Do you know when to call for assistance?*

A week after I returned from that hospital visit in December, Vincent's parents appeared at school. Vincent had not been feeling well and he had been cutting school. The night before, Vincent confessed to his mother that he didn't want to live.

I called for Vincent and waited for him in the hallway. I could see him from a distance, and he saw me but didn't speed or slow his walking pace. Instead, he hi-fived a friend and glanced into the bathroom. I could see his gelled hair carefully spiked into a patent leather crown, and his glowing orange shoelaces that he'd matched meticulously to an orange collared shirt. He was in dress code and that telegraphed to me that he cared about school and authority. However, the colors he chose telegraphed something else entirely. I tried hard to remember if that shade of orange was a gang color. He presented a complicated series of nested symbols.

I approached to greet him.

"Am I in trouble?" he asked.

"No," I told him and invited him into my office.

Inside, at my small round table were his parents and sister, the dean, and the guidance counselor.

His father begged, "Vincent, tell us what's bothering you."

There was a lot bothering Vincent. His oldest sister was pregnant with her second child. His 16-year-old sister had left high school. Mom had found a bandana in his backpack. The guidance counselor asked gently, firmly, and knowingly about his initiation to a gang, which seemed to have started with minor stealing and ended there. We learned Vincent was going to start therapy and the guidance counselor advised him to share his thoughts and trust in confidentiality. Vincent teared up as his mother started to cry about him, as well as the direction in which all her children were headed.

Vincent's father asked, "Why, Vincent, why?"

After the meeting during which Vincent's parents agreed to take him to outside counseling, I pulled up Vincent's school data. New York City has an Internet-based system, Achievement Reporting and Innovation System, nicknamed ARIS. It began as a complicated

cumbersome program but had been redesigned to provide a child's school history (attendance, numbers for
every test taken and report cards) on one tidy color
coded screen. ARIS gives a 21st-century meaning to
the notion of "permanent record." I viewed Vincent's
testing history from the time he entered the school system until the present. I could see his attendance, with
specific dates for absence. I could see he was a former
English language learner, and I viewed his seventh grade
transcript. Vincent's English language arts tests scores
were classic fence-sitter performance, for my school
community anyway. Depending on the year, Vincent
would be one question into the area of "meeting standards" or miss one question in the "approaching standards" rating. His report revealed no grade above a 70
in the two years he'd been at our school.

Vincent's urgency seemed to subside for a while until
he came to my office with his second quarter report
card. He was failing everything. Somehow the therapy,
the parental concern, the attention of the professionals
around him at school, and his teachers had still let him
slip away. Who was watching the store as we were robbed
blind? I knew as soon as I saw that report card, with
many grades below 60, that his recovery would be difficult. No, rather, I knew he was never going to pass and
knew that he knew it, too. We both knew mid year that
the year was over. We calculated the grades he needed to
achieve an "85" in nearly every subject.

"Vincent," I said. "Do you know how to get an 85?"

"No," he replied.

Why was Vincent's answer "no"? Why would the answer be "no" for so many of our students? Didn't his teachers tell him what they wanted? Didn't his teachers provide rubrics and show him how the descriptors translated into actual student work? Why hadn't he internalized the message of ambition, achievement, of personal standards, of success? Why wasn't he afraid of the repercussions of not doing his homework? Furthermore, why were so many other kids not getting this message? Perhaps they were getting other, louder messages from elsewhere.

Why, why, why is one of the conversational protocols on our data team. Why is it so cool to fail? Why do kids think failing school is the direct route to popularity? Why is it all right not to do homework, read, or be informed? Why do so many adolescents have low expectations of themselves? Why is it acceptable to come to school unprepared? Why do boys think it's girlish to read? Why do so many of my kids meet the NYS standards but risk academic failure? Why is failure so appealing? Why does failure feel good to them, or rather, why do they like to feel perpetually bad? While these questions pertained to Vincent, they pointed at the pervasive underachieving culture of all of our general education classes. This attitude is what really hampers us as an educational entity from "achievement."

I thought of my visit to the transplant center. I thought of my own questions. *If you are given an assignment, do you know how to do it? Do you know when you are failing? Do you know what to do if you are failing? Do you know when to call for assistance?* I added one more: *Do you know how to be persistent?*

As the pressure mounts for school improvement, closing achievement gaps, and developing an educated generation, I wonder why, in schools, we think of education as a science with measureable goals and a collection of numerical data when, so often, education is an art. I wonder if schools, as a single cultural force, are enough to signal to the community at large that being successful in school is important—and personally satisfying. Learning sticks to us with emotion, laughter, love, and just the right amount of anxiety. Learning requires a human touch. Entire classes of students bond with a teacher, and it is through that positive, loving connection that learning—all types of learning—occurs.

Back at the picnic, the eighth graders are signing yearbooks and surreptitiously texting. Teachers are stepping between teenagers who are "grinding," dancing hip to hip. My principal worries about the possibility of rain, whether or not the kids have enough water to drink, and the neighbors. We keep a sharp ear to the DJ, hoping he keeps blasting sanitized versions of the eighth graders' favorite music. Outside, I'm reviewing the data; the students, no matter what the cushion they passed their courses by, are celebrating their developmental milestone. To me, a child's soul refuses to be digitized. A child's drive refuses to be assigned a number and logged into his or her permanent record. I cannot record the music of questioning, the song of curiosity, or the voice of reason, kindness, and persistence.

Vincent is inside now with the others. The guidance counselor has checked in with him. He's going to repeat the eighth grade, and the data will tell you that he's at an increased disposition to drop out of high school.

But, maybe not.

THE MARCH
ACCUSATION

Bruce L. Greene

I'M USED TO having people walk into my classroom in the middle of a lesson. I have never been unnerved by it. One time, a parent in a bathrobe delivered a forgotten lunch. On another occasion, a misguided pizza delivery person ambled in, right in the middle of a lesson on starvation during the Great Depression. I've had my share of frantic parents and heartbroken teenage lovers needing resolution *now*. Sometimes a routine day crumbled with the unexpected entrance of a desperate colleague. Mary broke up with her boyfriend and needed to talk. Nancy ran out of chalk—again. Joe forgot to ask for a ride to his mechanic and wanted to catch me before I left campus. Most days featured at least one arrogant student liar, meeting me halfway to the door, dripping with attitude, blind to the transparence they emit. Perhaps I'm a bit too lax, but I always figured one more person, with one more demand, wasn't going to make much of a difference. I can always take a moment to stop what I'm doing and find that video someone forgot to pick up at a more appropriate time.

A personal visit from an administrator, however, is something else entirely. Usually those interruptions are reserved for scheduled evaluation observations, or a face-to-face request to fill in for someone at short notice. Granted, it was only my second year under contract, but maybe I missed something. When none of those excuses seemed to be the cause for the principal to be standing sheepishly at my threshold, I was a bit confused.

Mr. Nelson was hard to miss. He filled the doorframe with his gray woolen suit and shiny brown oxfords. Jim Nelson, hardly a threatening figure, smiled politely, if not nervously. Always pleasant, it was still hard to believe he'd been the quarterback and captain of our school's football team 30 years earlier. I was in the process of debriefing a discussion exercise on the United Farm Workers Union, about ten minutes before the end of the class period. My students were anticipating lunch, but nevertheless engaged in the final moments of our work. Kevin Brown, known mostly for his athletic ability, was particularly impressive that day, making a nice comparison between the rights of agricultural workers and skilled workers.

"People have to realize," he said, "not everyone can do someone else's job, and just because it may not be considered skilled work, how else would people get food on their table? These workers are not only worthy of dignity, they are necessary."

"Can we continue this tomorrow?" Jessica chimed in.

"Definitely," I agreed. "We need to look at the relationship between workers' wages and the importance of their work. You guys have brought up a crucial point here, so think about who gets paid the highest wages in our culture for doing what, okay?"

Allowing me to finish this discussion and a final thought, Mr. Nelson then summoned me with his darting eyes. Sky blue, they seemed to grow sharper and radiate like a laser beam in my direction. We were clearly in different generations. My black Levis and plaid shirts always contrasted sharply with whatever suit he wore. Even Mr. Nelson's striped ties were narrow and subdued. After all, it was 1974 and he was the principal of one of the largest high schools in the East Bay Area. I asked the class to return to their seats, and prepare to end for the day. They knew something was up. With seven minutes remaining, most of the class was more than happy to play the role of mature student just so they could see what prompted the principal's appearance. Kevin, however, was still feeling the moment and had no trouble making the transition from classroom discussion to real world. His broad grin abated. He mulled over the possibility of speaking then opted to pat down and pick the Afro he wore. Ten seconds later, he changed his mind.

"This is about his job, isn't it?" he barked at Mr. Nelson.

I walked to the door. Mr. Nelson slowly approached and handed me an envelope. Just then it clicked. March 15, that date meant something more than the Ides of March. Yet it was an omen nonetheless. I thought, this is what it's like to get a layoff notice. I'd heard rumors for months about impending pink slips. Our union representative even mentioned at the last faculty meeting that our local affiliate would be on hand to defend anyone, should hearings take place. My AFT affiliate had lost the collective bargaining election the year before, but I was assured that the NEA chapter that now represented my district would go to bat for all those who received layoff notices. It all seemed so foreign to me, so unnecessary, like the appearances I was forced to make before my draft board. Motioning me closer, Mr. Nelson whispered in my ear.

"Sorry to have to do it this way, but I've legally got to get these out before the end of the day. I have three more to deliver before the period ends. Wish I could stay and handle questions, but that will have to wait till the faculty meeting this afternoon."

"I'm fine," I reassured him. "I guess the middle of March just snuck up on me."

That's right. There are time constraints, dates, hearings, and appeals to consider when teachers get layoff notices. Mr. Nelson's departure emboldened my students.

"What's that, what's it say...? Ooohhh you're in trouble now huh, Mista Greene,"

Sophia joked, enjoying the moment a little too much. I unfolded the three-page legal document tucked in a school district envelope. Notice of Accusation, it read. Funny name I thought, but then these legal documents often have layers of meaning.

"It's a Notice of Accusation," I responded, beginning to chuckle. As is often the case, the kids took me at my word. I knew I needed to be careful throwing that word around. It reminded me of the time I told a student that Pringles potato chips were made on a Xerox machine; that's why they all looked alike. Three days later, when he still believed me and kept eagerly sharing this information with everyone, I knew that I'd better reign in my sense of humor.

"What are you being accused of?" three students simultaneously shouted.

Another chimed in, "I told you he was in trouble."

"I'm being accused of having a job, or maybe wanting my job, I guess."

The class was angry now. They knew about the impending layoffs. They also knew that the youngest teachers, along with electives such as the ethnic studies class they were in, would be on the block, as well. They knew that if I went, the History of Minorities in America classes went with me. New electives, like young teachers, share a similar vulnerability.

"No really," I explained, "that's what this document is called, a Notice of Accusation. It's a legal term, but it sure doesn't feel good. I feel like the blame is being placed on me."

The Sixth Amendment to the Constitution gives any person accused of a crime the right to self-defense. The plaintiff is legally bound to inform the defendant so that legal due process follows. It's very important. In a classroom with 32 warm bodies, it's also rather cold. *This is a legal matter,* I kept telling myself. *It involves protocols, hearings, and administrative law judges. It's about budget cuts and seniority lists, and not the human beings behind the numbers. Even so, why do I have to be served these papers in front of a class? Surely there must be a better way.*

Over the next decade, I came to realize that the document is aptly named. I was being terminated, against my wishes, my students, wishes, my students' parents' wishes, my colleagues' wishes, so I was entitled to my rights. After all, wasn't this a democracy? Didn't I, as a citizen and taxpayer, have rights? The accusation meant that I could defend myself. Yet it literally meant that I had been accused of a crime. Really: look at the legal definition. An accusation was being brought against me.

That's all I needed. On top of curriculum meetings, faculty meetings, department meetings, lessons to plan, papers to grade, parents to call, students to counsel, recommendation letters to write, books to read, exercise, grocery shopping, and sleep (forget personal life), I had to defend myself for wanting this to continue. Nevertheless, I did, of course, want just that. Add to the list substitute lessons to plan and that I needed to attend the hearings that legally took place.

By the time June rolled around, and the school year ground to a halt, I had one final obligation. After all the papers, projects, and exams were graded, after all the boxes were packed and books shelved, after all the decisions about what to take home and what to leave behind, I had one last thing left on my list. If I wanted to collect unemployment insurance for the summer. I was legally entitled to apply.

One overcast summer morning in late June, I made my way to the closest unemployment office. There, in the line that formed outside the building, before the doors opened for business, was Kevin Brown, the young man who had been in my classroom only days before. He chose the same day to register with the Department of Human Resources. How remarkable I thought. Only days earlier, we were on opposite ends of the spectrum. I knew I'd have a reasonably good chance of being rehired, but for the moment we were both standing in Square One. *I guess Kevin was serious about getting a summer job right away,* I thought. *I wonder if my predicament had any impact on him. He's registering for work, and I'm registering because I lost work.*

"You still need to consider college," I chided.

"Yeah, I know, but I gotta register here anyway because I need to make some money for later on first," he replied.

"That's f'ed up," he continued. "Why they gotta treat you like that? Why don't they let students decide who gets laid off?"

I reminded Kevin that it doesn't work that way and thanked him for the empathy.

"I'll probably get re-hired," I reassured him. "It's just that I have to go all summer without knowing. Then if I apply somewhere else and another offer comes along, I have to decide if I want to wait it out or not. There's got to be a better way; it is f'ed up."

We wished each other well, fighting off the silent conversation going on in our minds. I knew I'd have jobs to apply for by the end of the summer. If I couldn't return to my school, perhaps I'd receive an offer elsewhere in the district. However, Kevin had a longer road to travel. I hoped my plight wouldn't deter him from following his dreams. I knew it wouldn't deter me.

That was the first of three sets of layoff hearings I would attend in my first ten years of teaching. In time, the sting of Notices of Accusation lessened, as did my anxiety over them. Nevertheless, as I returned home that early summer day, the question still echoed in my ear, "What are you being accused of?"

ABOUT THE EDITOR

MAUREEN PICARD ROBINS is currently a middle school assistant principal and is a national presenter on education topics. She has presented for the National Staff Development Council on brain-based pedagogies to maximize student achievement and on the use of data for the purposes of school improvement. She also presented for the CEL branch of the National Council of the Teachers of English. Robins has presented to mentors and been involved with mentor training programs. She has presented to her city-wide English Assistant Principals and staff developers and is a frequently requested speaker.

Robins has written essays about education and family for national outlets such as the *New York Daily News*, MSNBC, and *Family Circle*, as well as book reviews for *The New York Times*. She also has co-authored a book with Dr. Sidney Trubowitz, *The Good Teacher Mentor*, published by Teachers College Press in 2003.

Prior to becoming an assistant principal, Robins was a literacy staff developer with particular expertise in the teaching of writing. Robins has a Masters of Educational Administration and a Masters in English.

ABOUT THE CONTRIBUTORS

SUSAN R. ADAMS is a former high school Spanish and ESL teacher and instructional coach in Indianapolis. Currently she is working at the College of Education at Butler University as the Project Alianza Title III grant manager, where she teaches professional development courses for practicing mainstream secondary teachers and works with university faculty to prepare teachers better to teach English language learners. Susan is pursuing a PhD in language education at Indiana University and is a teacher consultant with the Hoosier Writing Project, the local site for The National Writing Project.

LELAC ALMEGOR teaches seventh grade English at KIPP DC: AIM Academy.

TIM CLIFFORD is an education writer and the author of many children's books. He has two wonderful daughters and two energetic Border Collies that he adopted from a shelter. Tim became a vegetarian because of his love of animals. He is also a computer nut and a sports fanatic. He lives and works in New York City as a public school teacher.

SANDRA COHEN teaches math at the Frank Sinatra High School of the Arts in New York City. She has two adult children and is a proud grandma.

CHRISSY CORBISIERO is a graduate of Cornell University. She began as a New York City teaching fellow working in special education (District 75) in Harlem and Washington Heights. She then went on to teach special education in a community school in Queens. She is currently a private educator for a family in Manhattan.

BRYAN RIPLEY CRANDALL is a doctoral student in reading and language arts at Syracuse University. He spent over 10 years in Louisville, Kentucky, teaching high school English at the J. Graham Brown School, participating as a teacher fellow for the Louisville Writing Project, collaborating with the State Department of Education on the Writing Advisory Council, and enjoying an overseas collaboration with the Roskilde Lile Skole in Denmark. Crandall has been honored as an English Speaking Union Cambridge University Teacher Scholar, as a Fulbright Memorial Teaching Scholar in Japan, and as a Humana Bread Loaf School of English Teacher Scholar. Currently, he is enjoying his academic studies and his volunteer work with the Syracuse Sudanese Lost Boys Cow Project.

MARY ANN ELLIS has taught in Georgia for 32 years. She still loves teaching, especially literature and writing. She attended Georgia Southern Writing Project Summer Institute in 2002, and changed her teaching style completely and for the better. Discussing literature and sharing writings with students have, in her opinion, kept her young. For fun she writes a weekly column for *The Baxley News-Banner* and sponsors The Crow's Nest, a student page in the newspaper. When she does retire, she hopes to write full time.

DIANA GARCIA has taught for 14 years in Austin, currently working with English language learners. She is National Board Certified and has had much professional development in writing. When not teaching, she makes mail art, plays bass and drums, and volunteers for the Austin Baha'is or Girls Rock Camp Austin.

BRUCE GREENE taught for 33 years at an urban high school in the San Francisco Bay Area. As a teacher-consultant for the Bay Area Writing Project at UC Berkeley for the last 20 years, he's published numerous articles on educational issues in his own practice, as well as personal essays based on his experiences and observations. Bruce now lives and writes in Portland, Oregon. He is currently looking for an agent for his recently completed memoir, *Above This Wall: The Life and Times of a VISTA Volunteer 1969-70*.

FRED HAAS is a high school English teacher in the Boston suburbs, teaching classes both in person and online. A late arrival to teaching, he previously worked in the theatre and film industries, as well as spending years as a technology consultant. While focusing on education technology, as a consultant, he specialized in software training and broadband network video, in the days before YouTube. In addition to teaching, he serves as the technology liaison for the Boston Writing Project.

DEAN P. JOHNSON is in his 19th year of teaching. He has taught middle school, high school, community college, and university levels. For the past nine years he has been teaching English in Camden, New Jersey, a high poverty urban setting—currently listed as the second most dangerous city in the United States. He is also an adjunct at Rowan University where he teaches creative writing.

KELLY NORRIS is an English teacher at Minnechaug Regional High School in Wilbraham, Massachusetts. She is also the founding advisor of a club designed to support students of color and promote awareness of African American history and culture. She continues to learn about equity in the classroom and recently helped organize a workshop for teachers centered on anti-racism. Her essay is part of a larger work-in-progress exploring issues of race.

WIN RADIGAN has been an educator for nearly 40 years in a career spanning high school English teacher to assistant superintendent. Currently she serves as an educational consultant where she works with classroom teachers, supervisors, principals, and district staff developers in the areas of curriculum, instruction, and leadership.

EBONY ELIZABETH THOMAS is a doctoral candidate in the Joint Program in English and Education at the University of Michigan. Her research interests include teacher professional development, discourse analysis, multicultural education, and children's and young adult literature. Before she was in the world of higher education, Ebony taught elementary, middle, and high school for seven years, including one year as lead teacher for grade 5. She has presented her work at the National Association of Teachers of English, National Association for Multicultural Education, and the Children's Literature Association, as well as on the local and state level. Her work has appeared in *English Journal, Sankofa: A Journal of African Children's and Young Adult Literature,* and in the anthology *A Narrative Compass: Women's Scholarly Journeys.* In her spare time, Ebony enjoys baking, gardening, fitness, and cross-stitch.

VIVIANE VERSTANDIG has been a New York City educator for 21 years. Her experience includes working as an elementary classroom teacher and district level staff developer. She is currently the literacy coach in a Pre K–8 elementary/middle school. In addition, she is an adjunct professor at Queens College working in the master of arts in teaching program.

IT'S NOT ALL FLOWERS AND SAUSAGES

by Mrs. Mimi (as created by Jennifer Scoggin)

AVAILABLE WHEREVER BOOKS ARE SOLD!

M Y NAME IS Mrs. Mimi and I am a second-grade teacher in Harlem.

"Hi, Mrs. Mimi!"

When I tell people what I do for a living, I usually get one of three reactions.

Reaction #1: "Oooooo...little kids are sooooo cuuuuute! I am so jealous! It must be so fun to color and sing all day."

This reaction tends to send me into a bit of a rage, compelling me to regale these individuals with an insanely long laundry list of roles that teachers must balance. I feel the need to inform them of the incredible amount of planning and thought that goes into our days and point out that, unlike those who work in an office, I must complete all my daily tasks while simultaneously holding my own pee for eight hours at a time. *Eight hours!*

Reaction #2: "If I could spend some time volunteering, I would definitely work with children like you do."

Ummmm, moron, teachers get *paid* because we work *insanely hard.* But that's cool, I know you're really online shopping all day in your air-conditioned cubicle and are just feeling incredibly unfulfilled and worthless. Just try not to take it out on teachers next time, okay?

Reaction #3: "Wow! You work there?! You're totally like Michelle Pfeiffer in *Dangerous Minds*!"

Okay. No...just no.

I won't even respond to those who immediately point out that it must be nice to have my summers off. I feel as if they should just be shot.

(Note: Before continuing to read, please begin humming a song you think of as fairly badass. I find that having my own soundtrack helps make me feel even more fabulous than I already am. I mean, don't all inner-city public school teachers have their own soundtrack that follows them around? And wear lots of leather? Yes? No?)

Okay. So now that we've gotten *that* out of the way...

If I could, I would scream, "I am a teacher!" proudly from the highest mountain, but high heels do not lend themselves to intense hikes. Nor do I lend *myself* to anything quite so outdoorsy. Plus, screaming from a mountaintop just seems so cliché. And when you're a teacher, let's face it, there's practically a jungle of clichés for you to fight through, hence the ridiculous reactions I receive from those outside of the world of education when I tell them about my choice of career. Like I said, I don't do outside and I certainly don't do cliché. Let's take a look at some of these awfully inaccurate teacher clichés and poke some holes in them, shall we? Because I don't see myself represented anywhere...

Well, first we have the stereotypical image of an elementary school teacher who loves terrible thematic sweaters, sensible shoes, and necklaces made exclusively from dried pasta products and Tempra paint. This teacher may also be sporting some sort of dangly thematic earring that may or may not blink. Perhaps she is brandishing a pointer as well. I think this teacher's soundtrack might include hits from artists such as Raffi. Fortunately, she exists mainly in the cloudy, and very delusional, childhood memories of the classroom held by many who seem to think they went to school in a Norman Rockwell painting or something. I resent this teacher on many levels. But perhaps what I find most insulting is she is portrayed as a smiling idiot who is completely void of any sort of sass. She's just so...well, I think the macaroni necklace says it all.

I teach elementary school and somehow manage to dress myself every day without resorting to anything that can be purchased at the grocery store. In all honesty, I think of myself (and my school wardrobe) as pretty fabulous. And while I may not have a lithium-induced smile plastered on my face and Raffi blasting from my room, I do love my little friends. A lot. So much so, that I have a hard time leaving school at school and often hear myself continuing to talk about the adventures in my classroom long after my friends go home at 3. And, if I'm not talking *about* my students, I'm talking to other adults as if *they were* my students. Like at home with my husband, Mr. Mimi, I might find myself saying something like, "Honey, is that really where you want to leave your shoes? Do we want this to be a place where people have to worry about tripping over shoes left all over?" Yeah, I think it's safe to say Mr. Mimi loves (read: tolerates) this little habit of mine. I've tried to reform, but there's something about spending the entire day with 20 small people who quickly become more like a little family that makes it hard to leave it all behind in the classroom. I have never thought of teaching as just a job.

Okay. For our next cliché, we have the kind of teacher made popular by many a sitcom. This teacher appears to have insane amounts of free time during the school day. She spends the majority of this free time hanging out in the mahogany-furnished teachers' lounge. This lounge is usually also equipped with stainless steel appliances and could not be a further cry from the sad, mouse-poo–encrusted little microwave shoved in the corner of one of my colleague's classrooms. (Yeah, my colleague drew the short straw.) This teacher, who is usually wearing a very low-cut and entirely dry-clean-only outfit, can be seen furrowing her brow with concern at a passing student approximately a nanosecond before she begins flirting with the abundance of hot male teachers at her school. Her soundtrack would have a variety of Top 40 hits such as "Sexy Back" and "Promiscuous Girl." Again, she seems to have nowhere else to be. Yet somehow, back in reality, I never have any free time and spend most of my precious minutes alone running around the classroom, you know, doing stuff for the children? But hey, I guess we all have our priorities.

Let me be clear about something here. I never have a free minute between the hours of 8 and 3. Never. Ever. Having the time to pee feels like a luxury most days.

And finally, we have the overly done stereotype of the urban schoolteacher who is clad in extremely form-fitting leather. Her soundtrack is comprised of exclusively gangsta rap with the exception of that one heart-wrenching song of triumph. This song is reserved for the precise moment in which she successfully reaches every child and turns each of their lives around. This teacher can be imagined braving the harsh city streets armed with only a pen and her own smug determination. Although I think she is intended to inspire, she typically sends me into spastic fits of anger. I mean, first of all, leather is totally not practical for an environment in which there is no control over the thermostat. I mean, the average year-round temperature of my classroom is a balmy 86 degrees. And second of all, you're setting the rest of us up to fail, sister friend! I mean, *every* child is a success story? Those are dangerous stats…hero-complex much?

Like I said earlier, I teach in Harlem and am proud to say that I have never worn leather anywhere but on my feet. I am also proud to say that I have been fairly successful during my time there. However, I will never say that I have reached every child. In fact, on many an occasion, I know that I have failed them. Sometimes they are small failures, like when I dodge a conversation about farts by telling students to "just go get a drink of water and sit back down." And sometimes they are larger failures, like when I just can't find a way to help a child to make a year's worth of progress in reading. That's honest. But that is just a part of teaching, a very real part that my leather-wearing friend seems to have completely bypassed or conveniently ignored.

I guess all of these clichés have their place. I can even find them somewhat entertaining once I get past all of the aspects of these women that are blatantly offensive and mock my profession. What really bothers me the most about all these clichés is that I don't see myself in any of these images. Where is all the petty drama over photocopies and bullshit meetings? Where is the administrative ridiculousness? And where is all the urine?

This book is part of my story of teaching. By no means is it the whole story. I'm not sure that would fit into one book, what with my flair for dramatic storytelling and the complexity that is the American public school classroom. Plus, I'm not done teaching, don't have all the answers, and definitely have a lot more to learn. So this is part of my story, for now. It grows out of my blog, the purpose of which was to give me an anonymous space to vent my frustrations and possibly give voice to some of the ridiculous hurdles to good teaching. I had to make it funny, or else I would be forced to scream into my pillow each and every night. Yet please keep in mind that this is a *story,* not a transcription, of my experiences in the classroom. Names have been changed, characters have been collapsed, stories have been dramatized, and liberties have been taken. For real.

Let's not get it twisted. This book is not an attack on the places I have worked, nor is it aimed at the people with whom I have worked. You see, I don't work in a "bad school." At all. In fact, I work in a very good school, a school that has made a tremendous amount of progress and is making a truly positive difference in the lives of children. Seriously. *That* is what I think is so frustrating. I work in a "good school" with many hardworking people who are committed to change, yet the shenanigans you'll read about are still happening and interfering with progress.

This is a story (a hilarious story...if you ask me) of my life in the classroom and, ironically, how my little friends are often the people who save me when I think I'm drowning in a sea of administrative, organizational, and bureaucratic bull****.